Abbreviations

K = knit

K2tog = knit 2 stitches together

K3tog = knit 3 stitches together

M1 = make 1 (see "Special Instructions")

MB = make bobble (see "Special Instructions")

MK = make knot (see "Special Instructions")

MS = make star (see "Special Instructions")

P = purl

psso = pass slipped stitch over

p2sso = pass 2 slipped stitches over

P2tog = purl 2 stitches together

P3tog = purl 3 stitches together

P4tog = purl 4 stitches together

rep = repeat

sl = slip stitch purlwise unless otherwise instructed

st(s) = stitch(es)

St st = stockinette stitch (knit 1 row; purl 1 row)

tog = together

wyib = with yarn in back

wyif = with yarn in front

yb = yarn back

yf = yarn forward

YO = yarn over

Bamboo Stitch

Multiple of 2
Row 1: *YO, K2, pass YO over K2; rep from * to end.
Row 2: Purl.
Rep these 2 rows.

DECEMBER
31

Special Instructions

Cable 3 left:
Slip the next stitch onto a cable needle and hold at the front of your work, knit the next 2 stitches from the left-hand needle; then knit the stitch from the cable needle.

Cable 3 right:
Slip the next 2 stitches onto a cable needle and hold at the back of your work, knit the next stitch from the left-hand needle; then knit the 2 stitches from the cable needle.

Cable 4 back or cable 4 front:
Slip the next 2 stitches onto a cable needle and hold at the back (or front) of your work, knit the next 2 stitches from the left-hand needle; then knit the 2 stitches from the cable needle.

Cable 6 back or cable 6 front:
Slip the next 3 stitches onto a cable needle and hold at the back (or front) of your work, knit the next 3 stitches from the left-hand needle; then knit the 3 stitches from the cable needle.

Waving Rib Pattern

Multiple of 6 + 2

Row 1 (right side): P2, *K4, P2; rep from * to end.
Row 2: K2, *P4, K2; rep from * to end.
Row 3: Rep Row 1.
Row 4: Rep Row 2.
Row 5: K3, P2, *K4, P2; rep from * to last 3 sts, K3.
Row 6: P3, K2, *P4, K2; rep from * to last 3 sts, P3.
Row 7: Rep Row 5.
Row 8: Rep Row 6.
Rep these 8 rows.

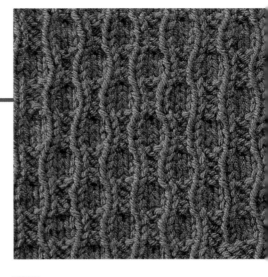

DECEMBER
30

Cable 8 back or cable 8 front:
Slip the next 4 stitches onto a cable needle and hold at the back (or front) of your work, knit the next 4 stitches from the left-hand needle; then knit the 4 stitches from the cable needle.

Cable 10 back or cable 10 front:
Slip the next 5 stitches onto a cable needle and hold at the back (or front) of your work, knit the next 5 stitches from the left-hand needle; then knit the 5 stitches from the cable needle.

Cable 12 back or cable 12 front:
Slip the next 6 stitches onto a cable needle and hold at the back (or front) of your work, knit the next 6 stitches from the left-hand needle; then knit the 6 stitches from the cable needle.

Cross 2 back or cross 2 front:
Knit into the back (or front) of the 2nd stitch on the needle; then knit the first stitch, slipping both stitches off the needle at the same time.

Cross 2 left:
Slip the next stitch onto a cable needle and hold at the front of your work, knit the next stitch from the left-hand needle; then knit the stitch from the cable needle.

Cross 2 right:
Slip the next stitch onto a cable needle and hold at the back of your work, knit the next stitch from the left-hand needle; then knit the stitch from the cable needle.

Goblets

Multiple of 6 + 2

Row 1 (right side): P3, K2, *P4, K2; rep from * to last 3 sts, P3.

Row 2: K3, P2, *K4, P2; rep from * to last 3 sts, K3.

Row 3: Rep Row 1.

Row 4: Rep Row 2.

Row 5: P2, *K4, P2; rep from * to end.

Row 6: K2, *P4, K2; rep from * to end.

Row 7: Rep Row 5.

Row 8: Rep Row 6.

Row 9: Purl.

Row 10: Knit.

Rep these 10 rows.

DECEMBER
29

Cross 2 purl:
Purl into the front of the 2nd stitch on the needle; then purl the first stitch, slipping both stitches off the needle together.

Cross 3:
Knit into the front of the 3rd stitch on the needle; then knit the first stitch in the usual way, slipping this stitch off the needle. Now knit the 2nd stitch in the usual way, slipping the 2nd and 3rd stitches off the needle together.

Cross 3 back:
Slip the next stitch onto a cable needle and hold at the back of your work, knit the next 2 stitches from the left-hand needle; then knit the stitch from the cable needle.

Cross 3 front:
Slip the next 2 stitches onto a cable needle and hold at the front of your work, knit the next stitch from the left-hand needle; then knit the 2 stitches from the cable needle.

Cross 3 together:
Slip the next 2 stitches onto a cable needle and hold at the back of your work, knit the next stitch from the left-hand needle; then knit together the 2 stitches from the cable needle.

Cross 4 back:
Knit into the back of the 4th stitch on the needle; then knit the first stitch in the usual way, slipping this stitch off the needle. Now knit the 2nd and 3rd stitches in the usual way, slipping the 3rd and 4th stitches off the needle together.

Honeycomb Cable Stitch

Multiple of 4 + 2

Row 1 (right side): Knit.
Row 2: P2, *K2, P2; rep from * to end.
Row 3: Knit.
Row 4: Rep Row 2.
Row 5: K1, *cross 2 front, cross 2 back; rep from * to last st, K1.
Row 6: K2, *P2, K2; rep from * to end.
Row 7: Knit.
Row 8: Rep Row 6.
Row 9: Knit.
Row 10: Rep Row 6.
Row 11: K1, *cross 2 back, cross 2 front; rep from * to last st, K1.
Row 12: Rep Row 2.
Rep these 12 rows.

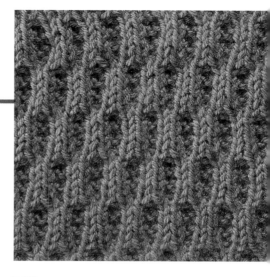

DECEMBER
28

Cross 4 front:
Knit into the front of the 4th stitch on the needle; then knit the first stitch in the usual way, slipping this stitch off the needle. Now knit the 2nd and 3rd stitches in the usual way, slipping the 3rd and 4th stitches off the needle together.

Cross 4 left:
Slip the next stitch onto a cable needle and hold at the front of your work, knit the next 3 stitches from the left-hand needle; then knit the stitch from the cable needle.

Cross 4 right:
Slip the next 3 stitches onto a cable needle and hold at the back of your work, knit the next stitch from the left-hand needle; then knit the 3 stitches from the cable needle.

Cross 6:
Slip the next 4 stitches onto a cable needle and hold at the front of your work, knit the next 2 stitches from the left-hand needle; then slip 2 stitches from the cable needle back to the left-hand needle. Pass the cable needle with the 2 remaining stitches to the back of your work, purl the 2 stitches from the left-hand needle; then knit the 2 stitches from the cable needle.

K1 in st below:
Insert the needle into the center of the stitch below the next stitch on the needle and knit in the usual way, slipping the stitch above it off the needle at the same time.

Textured Strip

Multiple of 3
Row 1 (right side): Knit.
Row 2: Purl.
Row 3: Knit.
Row 4: Purl.
Row 5: K1, *P1, K2; rep from * to last 2 sts, P1, K1.
Row 6: P1, *K1, P2; rep from * to last 2 sts, K1, P1.
Row 7: Rep Row 5.
Row 8: Rep Row 6.
Row 9: *P2, K1; rep from * to end.
Row 10: *P1, K2; rep from * to end.
Row 11: Rep Row 9.
Row 12: Rep Row 10.
Rep these 12 rows.

DECEMBER
27

Make 1:
Insert the left-hand needle from the back to the front into the horizontal strand of yarn lying between the stitch just worked and the next stitch. Knit through the front loop.

Make bobble:
(Purl 1, knit 1, purl 1, knit 1) all into the next stitch; pass the 2nd, 3rd, and 4th stitches over the first stitch.

Make knot:
Purl 3 stitches together, leaving the stitches on the left-hand needle. Wrap the yarn around the needle; then purl the same 3 stitches together again.

Make star:
See "Make knot."

Twist 2 left:
Slip the next stitch onto a cable needle and hold at the front of your work, purl the next stitch from the left-hand needle; then knit through the back loop of the stitch on the cable needle.

Twist 2 right:
Slip the next stitch onto a cable needle and hold at the back of your work, knit through the back loop of the next stitch on the left-hand needle; then purl the stitch from the cable needle.

Speckle Rib

Multiple of 2 + 1
Row 1 (right side): Knit.
Row 2: Purl.
Row 3: K1, *sl 1, K1; rep from * to end.
Row 4: K1, *sl 1 wyif, K1; rep from * to end.
Row 5: Knit.
Row 6: Purl.
Row 7: K2, *sl 1, K1; rep from * to last st, K1.
Row 8: K2, *sl 1 wyif, K1; rep from * to last st, K1.
Rep these 8 rows.

DECEMBER
26

Twist 3 back:
Slip the next stitch onto a cable needle and hold at the back of your work, knit the next 2 stitches from the left-hand needle; then purl the stitch from the cable needle.

Twist 3 front:
Slip the next 2 stitches onto a cable needle and hold at the front of your work, purl the next stitch from the left-hand needle; then knit the 2 stitches from the cable needle.

Twist 4 back:
Slip the next 2 stitches onto a cable needle and hold at the back of your work, knit the next 2 stitches from the left-hand needle; then purl the 2 stitches from the cable needle.

Twist 4 front:
Slip the next 2 stitches onto a cable needle and hold at the front of your work, purl the next 2 stitches from the left-hand needle; then knit the 2 stitches from the cable needle.

Twist 6 back:
Slip the next 3 stitches onto a cable needle and hold at the back of your work, knit the next 3 stitches from the left-hand needle; then purl the 3 stitches from the cable needle.

Twist 6 front:
Slip the next 3 stitches onto a cable needle and hold at the front of your work, purl the next 3 stitches from the left-hand needle; then knit the 3 stitches from the cable needle.

Rice Stitch

Multiple of 2 + 1
Row 1 (right side): P1, *K1 through back loop, P1; rep
from * to end.
Row 2: Knit.
Rep these 2 rows.

DECEMBER
25

Basket Rib

Multiple of 2 + 1
Row 1 (right side): Knit.
Row 2: Purl.
Row 3: K1, *sl 1 wyib, K1; rep from * to end.
Row 4: K1, *sl 1 wyif, K1; rep from * to end.
Rep these 4 rows.

JANUARY
1

Candle-Flame Stitch

Multiple of 4 + 2

Row 1 (right side): K2, *P2, K2; rep from * to end.

Row 2: P2, *K2, P2; rep from * to end.

Row 3: K2, *P2, cross 2 front; rep from * to last 4 sts, P2, K2.

Rows 4 and 5: Rep Row 2.

Row 6: Rep Row 1.

Row 7: P2, *cross 2 front, P2; rep from * to end.

Row 8: Rep Row 1.

Rep these 8 rows.

DECEMBER
24

Whelk Pattern

Multiple of 4 + 3
Row 1 (right side): K3, *sl 1 wyib, K3; rep from * to end.
Row 2: K3, *sl 1 wyif, K3; rep from * to end.
Row 3: K1, *sl 1 wyib, K3; rep from * to last 2 sts, sl 1 wyib, K1.
Row 4: P1, sl 1 wyif, *P3, sl 1 wyif; rep from * to last st, P1.
Rep these 4 rows.

JANUARY
2

Mini Bobble Stitch

Multiple of 2 + 1
Row 1 (right side): Knit.
Row 2: K1, *MB, K1; rep from * to end.
Row 3: Knit.
Row 4: K2, *MB, K1; rep from * to last st, K1.
Rep these 4 rows.

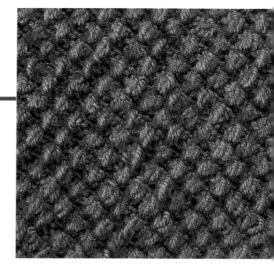

DECEMBER
23

Brick Rib

Multiple of 3 + 1

Row 1 (right side): *P2, K next st through back loop; rep from * to last st, P1.

Row 2: K1, *P next st through back loop, K2; rep from * to end.

Rows 3 and 4: Rep Rows 1 and 2.

Row 5: P1, *, K next 2 sts through back loop, P1; rep from * to end.

Row 6: K1, *P next 2 sts through back loop, K1; rep from * to end.

Rows 7 and 8: Rep Rows 5 and 6.

Row 9: P1, *K next st through back loop, P2; rep from * to end.

Row 10: *K2, P next st through back loop; rep from * to last st, K1.

Rows 11 and 12: Rep Rows 9 and 10.
Rep these 12 rows.

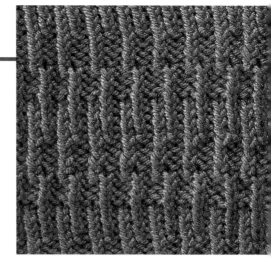

JANUARY
3

Reverse Stockinette Chevron

Multiple of 6 + 5
Row 1 (right side): K5, *P1, K5; rep from * to end.
Row 2: K1, *P3, K3; rep from * to last 4 sts, P3, K1.
Row 3: P2, *K1, P2; rep from * to end.
Row 4: P1, *K3, P3; rep from * to last 4 sts, K3, P1.
Row 5: K2, *P1, K5; rep from * to last 3 sts, P1, K2.
Row 6: Purl.
Rep these 6 rows.

DECEMBER
22

Zigzag Openwork

Multiple of 2 + 1
Row 1 (right side): K1, *K2tog; rep from * to end.
Row 2: K1, *YO, K1; rep from * to end.
Row 3: *K2tog; rep from * to last st, K1.
Row 4: Rep Row 2.
Rep these 4 rows.

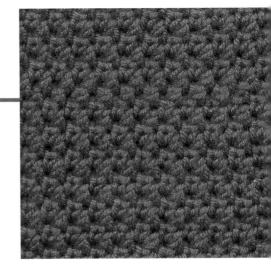

JANUARY
4

Elongated Chevron

Multiple of 18 + 1

Row 1 (right side): P1, *(K2, P2) twice, K1, (P2, K2) twice, P1; rep from * to end.

Row 2: K1, *(P2, K2) twice, P1, (K2, P2) twice, K1; rep from * to end.

Row 3: Rep Row 1.

Row 4: Rep Row 2.

Row 5: (P2, K2) twice, *P3, K2, P2, K2; rep from * to last 2 sts, P2.

Row 6: (K2, P2) twice, *K3, P2, K2, P2; rep from * to last 2 sts, K2.

Row 7: Rep Row 5.

Row 8: Rep Row 6.

Row 9: Rep Row 2.

Row 10: Rep Row 1.

Row 11: Rep Row 2.

Row 12: Rep Row 1.

Row 13: Rep Row 6.

Row 14: Rep Row 5.

Row 15: Rep Row 6.

Row 16: Rep Row 5.

Rep these 16 rows.

DECEMBER
21

Lacy Rib

Multiple of 3 + 1
Row 1 (right side): K1, *K2tog, YO, P1; rep from * to last 3 sts, K2tog, YO, K1.
Row 2: P3, *K1, P2; rep from * to last 4 sts, K1, P3.
Row 3: K1, YO, sl 1, K1, psso, *P1, YO, sl 1, K1, psso; rep from * to last st, K1.
Row 4: Rep Row 2.
Rep these 4 rows.

JANUARY
5

Honeycomb Stitch

Multiple of 4

Row 1 (right side): *Cross 2 front, cross 2 back; rep from * to end.

Row 2: Purl.

Row 3: *Cross 2 back, cross 2 front; rep from * to end.

Row 4: Purl.

Rep these 4 rows.

DECEMBER 20

Simple Lace Rib

Multiple of 6 + 1

Row 1 (right side): K next 2 sts through back loop, *K3, K next 3 sts through back loop; rep from * to last 5 sts, K3, K next 2 sts through back loop.

Row 2: P first 2 sts through back loop, *P3, P next 3 sts through back loop; rep from * to last 5 sts, P3, P next 2 sts through back loop.

Row 3: K first 2 sts through back loop, *YO, sl 1, K2tog, psso, YO, K next 3 sts through back loop; rep from * to last 5 sts, YO, sl 1, K2tog, psso, YO, K next 2 sts through back loop.

Row 4: Rep Row 2.

Rep these 4 rows.

JANUARY
6

Knot Pattern

Multiple of 6 + 5

Row 1 (right side): Knit.
Row 2: Purl.
Row 3: K1, *MK, K3; rep from * to last 4 sts, MK, K1.
Row 4: Purl.
Row 5: Knit.
Row 6: Purl.
Row 7: K4, *MK, K3; rep from * to last st, K1.
Row 8: Purl.
Rep these 8 rows.

DECEMBER
19

Crocus Buds

Multiple of 2 + 1

Row 1 (right side): K1, *YO, K2; rep from * to end.

Row 2: P1, *P3, pass 3rd st on right-hand needle over first 2 sts; rep from * to end.

Row 3: *K2, YO; rep from * to last st, K1.

Row 4: *P3, pass 3rd st on right-hand needle over first 2 sts; rep from * to last st, P1.

Rep these 4 rows.

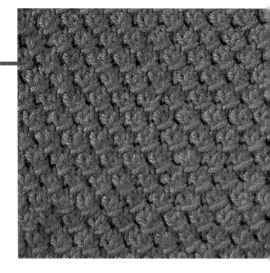

JANUARY
7

Little Shell Pattern

Multiple of 7 + 2
Row 1 (right side): Knit.
Row 2: Purl.
Row 3: K2, *YO, P1, P3tog, P1, YO, K2; rep from * to end.
Row 4: Purl.
Rep these 4 rows.

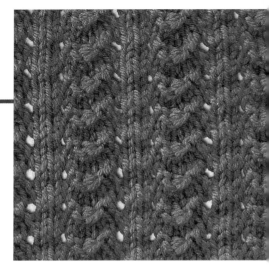

DECEMBER
18

Knotted Openwork

Multiple of 3

Row 1: Purl.

Row 2 (right side): K2, *YO, K3, pass 3rd st on right-hand needle over first 2 sts; rep from * to last st, K1.

Row 3: Purl.

Row 4: K1, *K3, pass 3rd st on right-hand needle over first 2 sts, YO; rep from * to last 2 sts, K2.

Rep these 4 rows.

JANUARY
8

Bee Stitch

Multiple of 2 + 1

Row 1: Knit.
Row 2 (right side): K1, *K1 in st below, K1; rep from * to end.
Row 3: Knit.
Row 4: K2, K1 in st below, *K1, K1 in st below; rep from * to last 2 sts, K2.
Rep these 4 rows.

DECEMBER 17

Tunnel Lace

Multiple of 3 + 2

Row 1 (right side): P2, *YO, K1, YO, P2; rep from * to end.

Row 2: K2, *P3, K2; rep from * to end.

Row 3: P2, *K3, P2; rep from * to end.

Row 4: K2, *P3tog, K2; rep from * to end.

Rep these 4 rows.

JANUARY
9

Berry Stitch

Multiple of 4 + 3

Row 1 (right side): K1, (K1, K1 through back loop, K1) into next st, *P3, (K1, K1 through back loop, K1) into next st; rep from * to last st, K1.

Row 2: K4, P3tog, *K3, P3tog; rep from * to last 4 sts, K4.

Row 3: K1, P3, *(K1, K1 through back loop, K1) into next st, P3; rep from * to last st, K1.

Row 4: K1, P3tog, *K3, P3tog; rep from * to last st, K1.
Rep these 4 rows.

DECEMBER
16

Herringbone Lace Rib

Multiple of 7 + 1
Row 1 (right side): K1, *P1, K1, YO, P2tog, K1, P1, K1; rep from * to end.
Row 2: P1, *K2, YO, P2tog, K2, P1; rep from * to end.
Rep these 2 rows.

JANUARY
10

Hindu Pillar Stitch

Multiple of 4 + 1

Row 1 (right side): K1, *P3tog without slipping sts from left-hand needle, knit them tog, then purl them tog, K1; rep from * to end.

Row 2: Purl.

Rep these 2 rows.

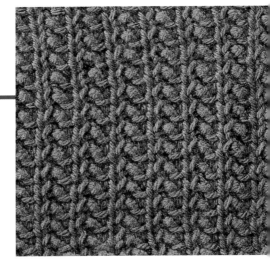

DECEMBER 15

Eyelets

Multiple of 3 + 2
Row 1 (right side): Knit.
Row 2: Purl.
Row 3: K2, *YO, K2tog, K1; rep from * to end.
Row 4: Purl.
Rep these 4 rows.

JANUARY
11

Loop Pattern

Multiple of 2
Row 1 (right side): Knit.
Row 2: * K1, sl 1; rep from * to last 2 sts, K2.
Row 3: Knit.
Row 4: K2, *sl 1, K1; rep from * to end.
Rep these 4 rows.

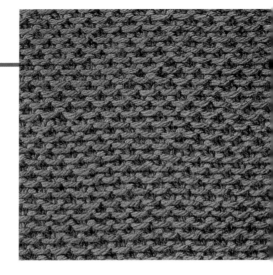

DECEMBER
14

Waterfall

Multiple of 6 + 3
Row 1 (right side): P3, *K3, YO, P3; rep from * to end.
Row 2: K3, *P4, K3; rep from * to end.
Row 3: P3, *K1, K2tog, YO, K1, P3; rep from * to end.
Row 4: K3, *P2, P2tog, K3; rep from * to end.
Row 5: P3, *K1, YO, K2tog, P3; rep from * to end.
Row 6: K3, *P3, K3; rep from * to end.
Rep these 6 rows.

JANUARY
12

Inverness Diamond

Multiple of 17

Row 1: P1, K3, P9, K3, *P2, K3, P9, K3; rep from * to last st, P1.

Row 2 (right side): K2, P3, K7, P3, *K4, P3, K7, P3; rep from * to last 2 sts, K2.

Row 3: P3, K3, P5, K3, *P6, K3, P5, K3; rep from * to last 3 sts, P3.

Row 4: K4, P3, K3, P3, *K8, P3, K3, P3; rep from * to last 4 sts, K4.

Row 5: P5, K3, P1, K3, *P10, K3, P1, K3; rep from * to last 5 sts, P5.

Row 6: K6, P5, *K12, P5; rep from * to last 6 sts, K6.

Row 7: P7, K3, *P14, K3; rep from * to last 7 sts, P7.

Row 8: K6, P5, *K12, P5; rep from * to last 6 sts, K6.

Row 9: Rep Row 5.

Row 10: Rep Row 4.

Row 11: Rep Row 3.

Row 12: Rep Row 2.

Rep these 12 rows.

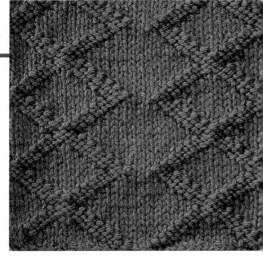

DECEMBER
13

Lacy Bubbles

Multiple of 6 + 3

Row 1 (right side): Purl.

Row 2: Knit.

Row 3: Purl.

Row 4: K1, P3tog, (K1, P1, K1, P1, K1) into next st,
*P5tog, (K1, P1, K1, P1, K1) into next st; rep from * to
last 4 sts, P3tog, K1.

Row 5: Purl.

Row 6: K1, (K1, P1, K1) into next st, P5tog, *(K1, P1,
K1, P1, K1) into next st, P5tog; rep from * to last 2 sts,
(K1, P1, K1) into next st, K1.

Row 7: Purl.

Row 8: Knit.

Rep these 8 rows.

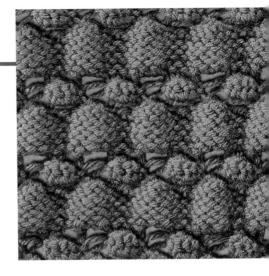

JANUARY
13

King Charles Brocade

Multiple of 12 + 1
Row 1 (right side): K1, *P1, K9, P1, K1; rep from * to end.
Row 2: K1, P1, K1, *P7, (K1, P1) twice, K1; rep from * to last 10 sts, P7, K1, P1, K1.
Row 3: (K1, P1) twice, *K5, (P1, K1) 3 times, P1; rep from * to last 9 sts, K5, (P1, K1) twice.
Row 4: P2, *K1, P1, K1, P3; rep from * to last 5 sts, K1, P1, K1, P2.
Row 5: K3, *(P1, K1) 3 times, P1, K5; rep from * to last 10 sts, (P1, K1) 3 times, P1, K3.
Row 6: P4, *(K1, P1) twice, K1, P7; rep from * to last 9 sts, (K1, P1) twice, K1, P4.
Row 7: K5, *P1, K1, P1, K9; rep from * to last 8 sts, P1, K1, P1, K5.
Row 8: Rep Row 6.
Row 9: Rep Row 5.
Row 10: Rep Row 4.
Row 11: Rep Row 3.
Row 12: Rep Row 2.
Rep these 12 rows.

DECEMBER
12

Lace and Cables

Multiple of 11 + 7

Row 1 (right side): K1, *YO, sl 1, K1, psso, K1, K2tog, YO, K6; rep from * to last 6 sts, YO, sl 1, K1, psso, K1, K2tog, YO, K1.

Row 2 and every even row: Purl.

Row 3: K2, *YO, sl 1, K2tog, psso, YO, K8; rep from * to last 5 sts, YO, sl 1, K2tog, psso, YO, K2.

Row 5: Rep Row 1.

Row 7: K2, *YO, sl 1, K2tog, psso, YO, K1, cable 6 back, K1; rep from * to last 5 sts, YO, sl 1, K2tog, psso, YO, K2.

Row 8: Rep Row 2.

Rep these 8 rows.

JANUARY
14

Diamond Brocade

Multiple of 8 + 1

Row 1 (right side): K4, *P1, K7; rep from * to last 5 sts, P1, K4.

Row 2: P3, *K1, P1, K1, P5; rep from * to last 6 sts, K1, P1, K1, P3.

Row 3: K2, *P1, K3; rep from * to last 3 sts, P1, K2.

Row 4: P1, *K1, P5, K1, P1, rep from * to end.

Row 5: *P1, K7; rep from * to last st, P1.

Row 6: Rep Row 4.

Row 7: Rep Row 3.

Row 8: Rep Row 2.

Rep these 8 rows.

DECEMBER
11

Fishtail Lace

Multiple of 8 + 1

Row 1 (right side): K1, *YO, K2, sl 1, K2tog, psso, K2, YO, K1; rep from * to end.

Row 2: Purl.

Row 3: K2, *YO, K1, sl 1, K2tog, psso, K1, YO, K3; rep from * to last 7 sts, YO, K1, sl 1, K2tog, psso, K1, YO, K2.

Row 4: Purl.

Row 5: K3, *YO, sl 1, K2tog, psso, YO, K5; rep from * to last 6 sts, YO, sl 1, K2tog, psso, YO, K3.

Row 6: Purl.

Rep these 6 rows.

JANUARY
15

Embossed Diamonds

Multiple of 10 + 3

Row 1 (right side): P1, K1, P1, *(K3, P1) twice, K1, P1; rep from * to end.

Row 2: P1, K1, *P3, K1, P1, K1, P3, K1; rep from * to last st, P1.

Row 3: K4, *(P1, K1) twice, P1, K5; rep from * to last 9 sts, (P1, K1) twice, P1, K4.

Row 4: P3, *(K1, P1) 3 times, K1, P3; rep from * to end.

Row 5: Rep Row 3.

Row 6: Rep Row 2.

Row 7: Rep Row 1.

Row 8: P1, K1, P1, *K1, P5, (K1, P1) twice; rep from * to end.

Row 9: (P1, K1) twice, *P1, K3, (P1, K1) 3 times; rep from * to last 9 sts, P1, K3, (P1, K1) twice, P1.

Row 10: Rep Row 8.

Rep these 10 rows.

DECEMBER
10

Ridged Lace 1

Multiple of 2 + 1

Rows 1–3: Purl.

Row 4 (right side): K1, *YO, sl 1, K1, psso; rep from * to end.

Rows 5–7: Purl.

Row 8: K1, *YO, K2tog; rep from * to end.

Rep these 8 rows.

JANUARY
16

Twisted Moss

Multiple of 2 + 1

Row 1: Knit.

Row 2 (right side): K1, *K1 in st below, K1; rep from * to end.

Row 3: Knit.

Row 4: K1 in st below, *K1, K1 in st below; rep from * to end.

Rep these 4 rows.

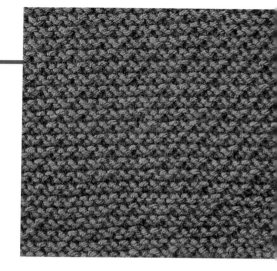

DECEMBER
9

Feather Lace

Multiple of 6 + 1

Row 1 (right side): K1, *YO, K2tog through back loop, K1, K2tog, YO, K1; rep from * to end.

Row 2 and every even row: Purl.

Row 3: K1, *YO, K1, sl 1, K2tog, psso, K1, YO, K1; rep from * to end.

Row 5: K1, *K2tog, YO, K1, YO, K2tog through back loop, K1; rep from * to end.

Row 7: K2tog, *(K1, YO) twice, K1, sl 1, K2tog, psso; rep from * to last 5 sts, (K1, YO) twice, K1, K2tog through back loop.

Row 8: Rep Row 2.

Rep these 8 rows.

JANUARY
17

Moss Slip Stitch

Multiple of 2 + 1

Row 1 (right side): K1, *sl 1, K1; rep from * to end.
Row 2: K1, *sl 1 wyif, K1; rep from * to end.
Row 3: K2, *sl 1, K1; rep from * to last st, K1.
Row 4: K2, *sl 1 wyif, K1; rep from * to last st, K1.
Rep these 4 rows.

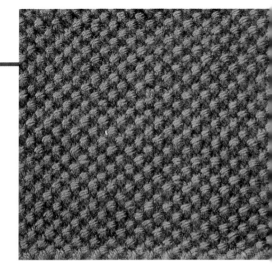

DECEMBER
8

Trellis Lace

Multiple of 6 + 5

Row 1 (right side): K4, *YO, sl 1, K2tog, psso, YO, K3; rep from * to last st, K1.

Row 2: Purl.

Row 3: K1, *YO, sl 1, K2tog, psso, YO, K3; rep from * to last 4 sts, YO, sl 1, K2tog, psso, YO, K1.

Row 4: Purl.

Rep these 4 rows.

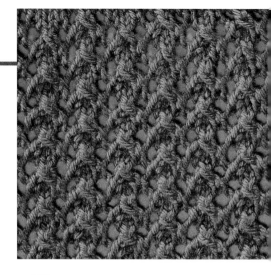

JANUARY
18

Moss-Stitch Zigzag

Multiple of 9
Row 1 (right side): *(K1, P1) twice, K4, P1; rep from * to end.
Row 2: *P4, (K1, P1) twice, K1; rep from * to end.
Row 3: (K1, P1) 3 times, *K4, (P1, K1) twice, P1; rep from * to last 3 sts, K3.
Row 4: P2, *(K1, P1) twice, K1, P4; rep from * to last 7 sts, (K1, P1) twice, K1, P2.
Row 5: K3, *(P1, K1) twice, P1, K4; rep from * to last 6 sts, (P1, K1) 3 times.
Row 6: *(K1, P1) twice, K1, P4; rep from * to end.
Row 7: Rep Row 5.
Row 8: Rep Row 4.
Row 9: Rep Row 3.
Row 10: Rep Row 2.
Rep these 10 rows.

DECEMBER
7

Eyelet Knot Stitch

Multiple of 2

Row 1 (right side): K1, *K2tog; rep from * to last st, K1.

Row 2: K2, *M1, K1; rep from * to end.

Row 3: Knit.

Row 4: Purl.

Rep these 4 rows.

JANUARY
19

Hunter's Stitch

Multiple of 11 + 4
Row 1 (right side): P4, *(K1 through back loop, P1) 3 times, K1 through back loop, P4; rep from * to end.
Row 2: K4, *P1 (K1 through back loop, P1) 3 times, K4; rep from * to end.
Rep these 2 rows.

DECEMBER
6

Rose-Hip Stitch

Multiple of 4 + 3

Row 1 (right side): K3, *sl 1 wyib, K3; rep from * to end.

Row 2: K3, *sl 1 wyif, K3; rep from * to end.

Row 3: K1, *sl 1 wyib, K3; rep from * to last 2 sts, sl 1 wyib, K1.

Row 4: K1, *sl 1 wyif, K3; rep from * to last 2 sts, sl 1 wyif, K1.

Rep these 4 rows.

JANUARY
20

Harris-Tweed Rib

Multiple of 4 + 2
Row 1 (right side): K2, *P2, K2; rep from * to end.
Row 2: P2, *K2, P2; rep from * to end.
Row 3: Knit.
Row 4: Purl.
Row 5: Rep Row 1.
Row 6: Rep Row 2.
Row 7: Purl.
Row 8: Knit.
Rep these 8 rows.

DECEMBER
5

Chevron

Multiple of 8 + 1
Row 1 (right side): K1, *P7, K1; rep from * to end.
Row 2: P1, *K7, P1; rep from * to end.
Row 3: K2, *P5, K3; rep from * to last 7 sts, P5, K2.
Row 4: P2, *K5, P3; rep from * to last 7 sts, K5, P2.
Row 5: K3, *P3, K5; rep from * to last 6 sts, P3, K3.
Row 6: P3, *K3, P5; rep from * to last 6 sts, K3, P3.
Row 7: K4, *P1, K7; rep from * to last 5 sts, P1, K4.
Row 8: P4, *K1, P7; rep from * to last 5 sts, K1, P4.
Row 9: Rep Row 2.
Row 10: Rep Row 1.
Row 11: Rep Row 4.
Row 12: Rep Row 3.
Row 13: Rep Row 6.
Row 14: Rep Row 5.
Row 15: Rep Row 8.
Row 16: Rep Row 7.
Rep these 16 rows.

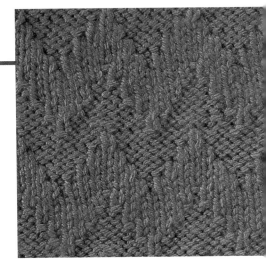

JANUARY
21

Cluster Rib

Multiple of 3 + 1
Row 1 (right side): P1, *K2, P1; rep from * to end.
Row 2: K1, *YO, K2, slip YO over the 2 knit sts, K1; rep from * to end.
Rep these 2 rows.

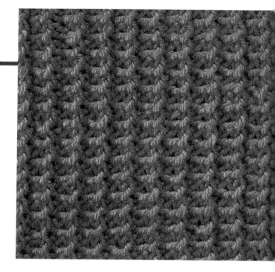

DECEMBER
4

Knotted Cords

Multiple of 6 + 5
Row 1 (right side): P5, *K1, P5; rep from * to end.
Row 2: K5, *P1, K5; rep from * to end.
Row 3: P5, *knit into front, back, and front of next st, P5; rep from * to end.
Row 4: K5, *P3tog, K5; rep from * to end.
Rep these 4 rows.

JANUARY
22

Garter Slip Stitch 3

Multiple of 2 + 1
Row 1 (wrong side): Knit.
Row 2: Knit.
Row 3: K1, *sl 1, K1; rep from * to end.
Row 4: Knit.
Rep these 4 rows.

DECEMBER
3

Organ Pipes

Multiple of 6 + 4

Row 1 (right side): K4, *P2, K4; rep from * to end.
Row 2: P4, *K2, P4; rep from * to end.
Row 3: Rep Row 1.
Row 4: Rep Row 2.
Row 5: P1, K2, *P4, K2; rep from * to last st, P1.
Row 6: K1, P2, *K4, P2; rep from * to last st, K1.
Row 7: Rep Row 5.
Row 8: Rep Row 6.
Row 9: Purl.
Row 10: Knit.

Rep these 10 rows.

JANUARY
23

Garter Slip Stitch 2

Multiple of 2 + 1

Row 1 (right side): Knit.
Row 2: Knit.
Row 3: K1, *sl 1, K1; rep from * to end.
Row 4: K1, *sl 1 wyif, K1; rep from * to end.
Rows 5 and 6: Knit.
Row 7: K2, *sl 1, K1; rep from * to last st, K1.
Row 8: K2, *sl 1 wyif, K1; rep from * to last st, K1.
Rep these 8 rows.

DECEMBER

2

Four-Stitch Cable 1

Worked on a background of reverse St st
Row 1 (right side): Knit.
Row 2: Purl.
Rows 3 and 4: Rep Rows 1 and 2.
Row 5: Cable 4 back.
Row 6: Purl.
Rep these 6 rows.

These instructions result in a cable that twists to the right (shown at right in photo). To twist the cable to the left (shown at left in photo), hold the cable to the front instead of the back in Row 5.

JANUARY
24

Garter Slip Stitch 1

Multiple of 2 + 1

Row 1 (right side): Knit.
Row 2: Knit.
Row 3: K1, *sl 1, K1; rep from * to end.
Row 4: K1, *sl 1 wyif, K1; rep from * to end.
Rep these 4 rows.

DECEMBER
1

Six-Stitch Cable

Worked on a background of reverse St st
Row 1 (right side): Knit.
Row 2: Purl.
Row 3: Cable 6 back.
Row 4: Purl.
Rep these 4 rows.

These instructions result in a cable that twists to the right (shown at right in photo). To twist the cable to the left (shown at left in photo), hold the cable to the front instead of the back in Row 3.

JANUARY
25

Traveling Ribbed Eyelet Panel

Worked over 13 sts on a background of St st

Row 1 (right side): K2, P2, YO, sl 1, K1, psso, K1, K2tog, YO, P2, K2.

Row 2: K4, P5, K4.

Rows 3–6: Rep Rows 1 and 2 twice.

Row 7: K2, P2, K5, P2, K2.

Row 8: Rep Row 2.

Row 9: K2, P2, K2tog, YO, K1, YO, sl 1, K1, psso, P2, K2.

Row 10: Rep Row 2.

Rows 11–14: Rep Rows 9 and 10 twice.

Row 15: Rep Row 7.

Row 16: Rep Row 2.

Rep these 16 rows.

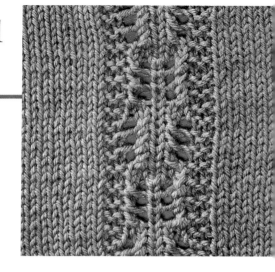

NOVEMBER
30

Eight-Stitch Cable

Row 1 (right side): Knit.
Row 2: Purl.
Rows 3 and 4: Rep Rows 1 and 2.
Row 5: Cable 8 back.
Row 6: Purl.
Rows 7–10: Rep Rows 1 and 2 twice more.
Rep these 10 rows.

These instructions result in a cable that twists to the right (shown at right in photo). To twist the cable to the left (shown at left in photo), hold the cable to the front instead of the back in Row 5.

JANUARY
26

Shetland Eyelet Panel

Worked over 9 sts on a background of St st

Row 1 (right side): K2, K2tog, YO, K1, YO, sl 1, K1, psso, K2.

Row 2 and every even row: Purl.

Row 3: K1, K2tog, YO, K3, YO, sl 1, K1, psso, K1.

Row 5: K1, YO, sl 1, K1, psso, YO, sl 2 knitwise, K1, p2sso, YO, K2tog, YO, K1.

Row 7: K3, YO, sl 2 knitwise, K1, p2sso, YO, K3.

Row 8: Rep Row 2.

Rep these 8 rows.

NOVEMBER
29

Little Lace Panel

Worked over 5 sts on a background of St st
Row 1 (right side): K1, YO, K3, YO, K1.
Row 2: Purl.
Row 3: K2, sl 1, K2tog, psso, K2.
Row 4: Purl.
Rep these 4 rows.

JANUARY
27

Staggered Fern Lace Panel

Worked over 20 sts on a background of St st

Row 1 (right side): P2, K9, YO, K1, YO, K3, sl 1, K2tog, psso, P2.

Row 2 and every even row: Purl.

Row 3: P2, K10, YO, K1, YO, K2, sl 1, K2tog, psso, P2.

Row 5: P2, K3tog, K4, YO, K1, YO, K3, (YO, K1) twice, sl 1, K2tog, psso, P2.

Row 7: P2, K3tog, K3, YO, K1, YO, K9, P2.

Row 9: P2, K3tog, K2, YO, K1, YO, K10, P2.

Row 11: P2, K3tog, (K1, YO) twice, K3, YO, K1, YO, K4, sl 1, K2tog, psso, P2.

Row 12: Rep Row 2.

Rep these 12 rows.

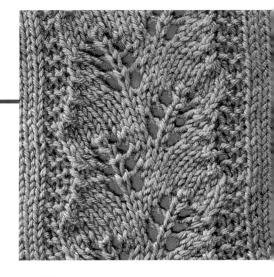

NOVEMBER
28

Faggoted Panel

Worked over 9 sts on a background of St st

Row 1 (right side): P1, K1, K2tog, YO, K1, YO, K2tog through back loop, K1, P1.

Row 2: K1, P7, K1.

Row 3: P1, K2tog, YO, K3, YO, K2tog through back loop, P1.

Row 4: Rep Row 2.

Rep these 4 rows.

JANUARY
28

Small Twist Pattern

Multiple of 8 + 6
Row 1 (right side): Knit.
Row 2 and every even row: Purl.
Row 3: K1, cable 4 front, *K4, cable 4 front; rep from
* to last st, K1.
Row 5: Knit.
Row 7: K5, cable 4 front, *K4, cable 4 front; rep from
* to last 5 sts, K5.
Row 8: Purl.
Rep these 8 rows.

NOVEMBER
27

Diamond Panel

Worked over 11 sts on a background of St st

Row 1 (right side): P2, K2tog, (K1, YO) twice, K1, sl 1, K1, psso, P2.

Row 2 and every even row: K2, P7, K2.

Row 3: P2, K2tog, YO, K3, YO, sl 1, K1, psso, P2.

Row 5: P2, K1, YO, sl 1, K1, psso, K1, K2tog, YO, K1, P2.

Row 7: P2, K2, YO, sl 1, K2tog, psso, YO, K2, P2.

Row 8: Rep Row 2.

Rep these 8 rows.

JANUARY
29

Thirteen-Stitch Claw Pattern

Done on a background of reverse St st

Upward Claw (shown at left in photo)
Row 1 (right side): Knit.
Row 2: Purl.
Row 3: Cable 6 back, K1, cable 6 front.
Row 4: Purl.
Rep these 4 rows.

Downward Claw (shown at right in photo)
Row 1 (right side): Knit.
Row 2: Purl.
Row 3: Cable 6 front, K1, cable 6 back.
Row 4: Purl.
Rep these 4 rows.

NOVEMBER
26

Leaf Panel

Worked over 24 sts on a background of St st

Row 1 (right side): Sl 1, K2tog, psso, K7, YO, K1, YO, P2, YO, K1, YO, K7, K3tog.

Row 2 and every even row: P11, K2, P11.

Row 3: Sl 1, K2tog, psso, K6, (YO, K1) twice, P2, (K1, YO) twice, K6, K3tog.

Row 5: Sl 1, K2tog, psso, K5, YO, K1, YO, K2, P2, K2, YO, K1, YO, K5, K3tog.

Row 7: Sl 1, K2tog, psso, K4, YO, K1, YO, K3, P2, K3, YO, K1, YO, K4, K3tog.

Row 9: Sl 1, K2tog, psso, K3, YO, K1, YO, K4, P2, K4, YO, K1, YO, K3, K3tog.

Row 10: Rep Row 2.

Rep these 10 rows.

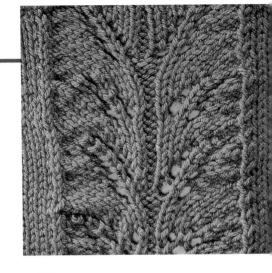

JANUARY
30

Loose Woven Cables

Multiple of 6 + 2

Row 1 (right side): Knit.

Row 2: K1, knit to last st wrapping yarn twice around needle for each st, K1.

Row 3: K1, *cable 6 back (dropping extra loops); rep from * to last st, K1.

Rows 4 and 5: Knit.

Row 6: K4, *knit to last 4 sts, wrapping yarn twice around needle for each st, K4.

Row 7: K4, *cable 6 front (dropping extra loops); rep from * to last 4 sts, K4.

Row 8: Knit.

Rep these 8 rows.

NOVEMBER
25

Wheatear Stitch

Multiple of 8 + 6

Row 1 (right side): P5, *K2, YO, sl 1, K1, psso, P4; rep from * to last st, P1.

Row 2: K5, *P2, YO, P2tog, K4; rep from * to last st, K1.

Rows 3–8: Rep Rows 1 and 2 three more times.

Row 9: P1, *K2, YO, sl 1, K1, psso, P4; rep from * to last 5 sts, K2, YO, sl 1, K1, psso, P1.

Row 10: K1, *P2, YO, P2tog, K4; rep from * to last 5 sts, P2, YO, P2tog, K1.

Rows 11–16: Rep Rows 9 and 10 three more times. Rep these 16 rows.

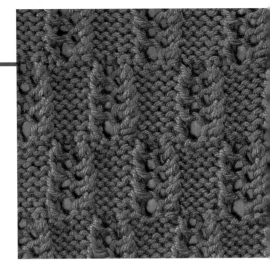

JANUARY
31

Forked Cable

Multiple of 8 + 2

Row 1: Purl.

Row 2 (right side): P3, K4, *P4, K4; rep from * to last 3 sts, P3.

Rows 3–7: Rep Rows 1 and 2 twice, then rep Row 1 again.

Row 8: K3, P4, *K4, P4; rep from * to last 3 sts, K3.

Row 9: Purl.

Row 10: K1, *cable 4 front, cable 4 back; rep from * to last st, K1.

Rep these 10 rows.

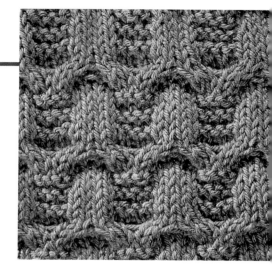

NOVEMBER
24

Flower Buds

Multiple of 8 + 5

Row 1 (right side): K3, *YO, K2, P3tog, K2, YO, K1; rep from * to last 2 sts, K2.

Row 2: Purl.

Rows 3–6: Rep Rows 1 and 2 twice more.

Row 7: K2, P2tog, *K2, YO, K1, YO, K2, P3tog; rep from * to last 9 sts, K2, YO, K1, YO, K2, P2tog, K2.

Row 8: Purl.

Rows 9–12: Rep Rows 7 and 8 twice more.

Rep these 12 rows.

FEBRUARY
1

Broken Chevron

Multiple of 12

Row 1 (right side): K1, P2, *K2, P2; rep from * to last st, K1.

Row 2: P1, K2, *P2, K2; rep from * to last st, P1.

Row 3: *P4, K2; rep from * to end.

Row 4: *P2, K4; rep from * to end.

Row 5: Rep Row 2.

Row 6: K1, P2, *K2, P2; rep from * to last st, K1.

Row 7: *K2, P6, K2, P2; rep from * to end.

Row 8: *K2, P2, K6, P2; rep from * to end.

Rows 9–14: Rep Rows 1–6.

Row 15: (P2, K2) twice, *P6, K2, P2, K2; rep from * to last 4 sts, P4.

Row 16: K4, P2, K2, P2, *K6, P2, K2, P2; rep from * to last 2 sts, K2.

Rep these 16 rows.

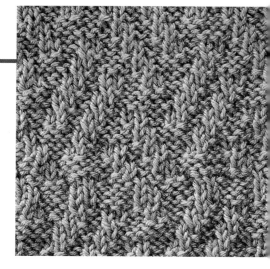

NOVEMBER
23

Snowdrop Lace

Multiple of 8 + 5

Row 1 (right side): K1, *YO, sl 1, K2tog, psso, YO, K5; rep from * to last 4 sts, YO, sl 1, K2tog, psso, YO, K1.

Row 2 and every even row: Purl.

Row 3: Rep Row 1.

Row 5: K4, *YO, sl 1, K1, psso, K1, K2tog, YO, K3; rep from * to last st, K1.

Row 7: K1, *YO, sl 1, K2tog, psso, YO, K1; rep from * to end.

Row 8: Rep Row 2.

Rep these 8 rows.

FEBRUARY
2

Simple Seed Stitch

Multiple of 4 + 1

Row 1 (right side): P1, *K3, P1; rep from * to end.
Row 2 and every even row: Purl.
Row 3: Knit.
Row 5: K2, P1, *K3, P1; rep from * to last 2 sts, K2.
Row 7: Knit.
Row 8: Repeat Row 2.
Rep these 8 rows.

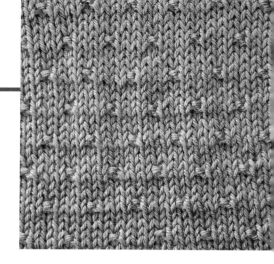

NOVEMBER
22

Tight Braid Cable

Worked over 10 sts on a background of reverse St st
Row 1: Purl.
Row 2 (right side): K2, (cable 4 front) twice.
Row 3: Purl.
Row 4: (Cable 4 back) twice, K2.
Rep these 4 rows.

FEBRUARY
3

Seed-Pearl Grid

Multiple of 8 + 1
Row 1 and every odd row: Purl.
Row 2 (right side): P1, *K1, P1; rep from * to end.
Row 4: Knit.
Row 6: P1, *K7, P1; rep from * to end.
Row 8: Knit.
Row 10: Rep Row 6.
Row 12: Knit.
Rep these 12 rows.

NOVEMBER
21

Garter Stitch Twisted Rib

Multiple of 4
Row 1 (right side): K1, *cross 2 back, K2; rep from * to last 3 sts, cross 2 back, K1.
Row 2: K1, *yf, cross 2 purl, yb, K2; rep from * to last 3 sts, yf, cross 2 purl, yb, K1.
Rep these 2 rows.

FEBRUARY
4

Slipped Three-Stitch Cable

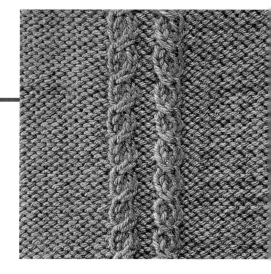

Done on a background of reverse St st

Slipped to the Right (shown at left in photo)
Row 1 (right side): K2, sl 1.
Row 2: Sl 1, P2.
Row 3: Cable 3 right.
Row 4: Purl.
Rep these 4 rows.

Slipped to the Left (shown at right in photo)
Row 1 (right side): Sl 1, K2.
Row 2: P2, sl 1.
Row 3: Cable 3 left.
Row 4: Purl.
Rep these 4 rows.

NOVEMBER
20

Contrary Fisherman's Rib

Multiple of 2 + 1

Foundation row: Knit.

Row 1 (right side): Sl 1, *K1 in st below, K1; rep from * to end.

Row 2: Sl 1, *K1, K1 in st below; rep from * to last 2 sts, K2.

Row 3: Rep Row 1.

Row 4: Rep Row 2.

Row 5: Rep Row 1.

Row 6: Sl 1, *K1 in st below, K1; rep from * to end.

Row 7: Rep Row 2.

Row 8: Rep Row 6.

Row 9: Rep Row 2.

Row 10: Rep Row 6.

Rep Rows 1–10 only.

FEBRUARY
5

Braided Cable

Worked over 9 sts on a background of reverse St st

Row 1: Twist 3 front, twist 3 back, twist 3 front.
Row 2: P2, K2, P4, K1.
Row 3: P1, cable 4 back, P2, K2.
Row 4: Rep Row 2.
Row 5: Twist 3 back, twist 3 front, twist 3 back.
Row 6: K1, P4, K2, P2.
Row 7: K2, P2, cable 4 front, P1.
Row 8: Rep Row 6.
Rep these 8 rows.

NOVEMBER
19

Mock Wavy Cable Rib

Multiple of 4 + 2

Row 1 (right side): P2, *K2, P2; rep from * to end.

Row 2 and every even row: K2, *P2, K2; rep from * to end.

Row 3: P2, *cross 2 back, P2; rep from * to end.

Row 5: Rep Row 1.

Row 7: P2, *K2tog but do not slip off needle, then insert right-hand needle between these 2 sts and knit first st again, slipping both sts off needle tog, P2; rep from * to end.

Row 8: Rep Row 2.

Rep these 8 rows.

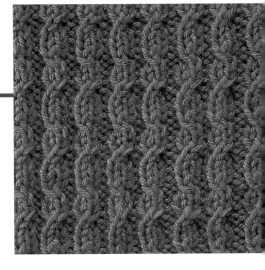

FEBRUARY
6

Little Pearl Cable

Worked over 4 sts on a background of reverse St st
Row 1 (right side): Cross 2 front, cross 2 back.
Row 2: Purl.
Row 3: Cross 2 back, cross 2 front.
Row 4: Purl.
Rep these 4 rows.

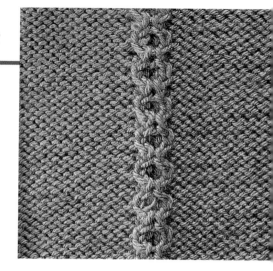

NOVEMBER
18

Slipped Rib 1

Multiple of 2 + 1

Row 1 (right side): K1, *sl 1 wyif, K1; rep from * to end.

Row 2: Purl.

Rep these 2 rows.

FEBRUARY
7

Six-Stitch Spiral Cable

Done on a background of reverse St st
Row 1 (right side): Cross 2 front 3 times.
Row 2: Purl.
Row 3: K1, cross 2 front twice, K1.
Row 4: Purl.
Rep these 4 rows.

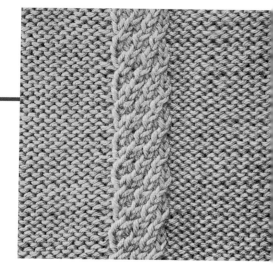

NOVEMBER
17

Feather Openwork

Multiple of 5 + 2
Row 1 (right side): K1, *K2tog, YO, K1, YO, sl 1, K1, psso; rep from * to last st, K1.
Row 2: Purl.
Rep these 2 rows.

FEBRUARY
8

Eyelet Cable

Multiple of 8 + 1

Row 1 (right side): P1, *cross 3 together, P1, K3, P1; rep from * to end.

Row 2: K1, *P3, K1, P1, YO, P1, K1; rep from * to end.

Row 3: P1, *K3, P1, cross 3 together, P1; rep from * to end.

Row 4: K1, *P1, YO, P1, K1, P3, K1; rep from * to end.

Rep these 4 rows.

NOVEMBER
16

Feather and Fan

Multiple of 18 + 2
Row 1 (right side): Knit.
Row 2: Purl.
Row 3: K1, *K2tog 3 times, (YO, K1) 6 times, K2tog
3 times; rep from * to last st, K1.
Row 4: Knit.
Rep these 4 rows.

FEBRUARY
9

Perforated Ribbing

Multiple of 6 + 3

Row 1 (right side): P1, K1, P1, *YO, P3tog, YO, P1, K1, P1; rep from * to end.

Row 2: K1, P1, K1, *P3, K1, P1, K1; rep from * to end.

Row 3: P1, K1, P1, *K3, P1, K1, P1; rep from * to end.

Row 4: Rep Row 2.

Rep these 4 rows.

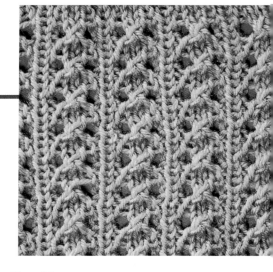

NOVEMBER
15

Pillar Openwork

Multiple of 3 + 2
Row 1 (right side): K1, *YO, sl 1, K2, psso the K2; rep
from * to last st, K1.
Row 2: Purl.
Rep these 2 rows.

Feather Rib

Multiple of 5 + 2
Row 1 (right side): P2, *YO, K2tog through back loop, K1, P2; rep from * to end.
Row 2: K2, *YO, K2tog through back loop, P1, K2; rep from * to end.
Rep these 2 rows.

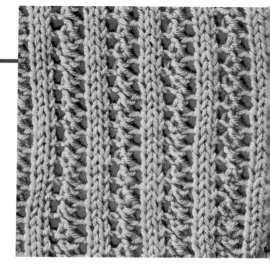

NOVEMBER
14

Little Fountain Pattern

Multiple of 4 + 1

Row 1 (right side): K1, *YO, K3, YO, K1; rep from * to end.

Row 2: Purl.

Row 3: K2, sl 1, K2tog, psso, *K3, sl 1, K2tog, psso; rep from * to last 2 sts, K2.

Row 4: Purl.

Rep these 4 rows.

FEBRUARY
11

Staggered Brioche Rib

Multiple of 2 + 1

Row 1: Knit.

Row 2 (right side): K1, *K1 in st below, K1; rep from * to end.

Rows 3–5: Rep Row 2 three more times.

Row 6: K2, K1 in st below, *K1, K1 in st below; rep from * to last 2 sts, K2.

Rows 7–9: Rep Row 6 three more times.

Rep Rows 2-8 throughout.

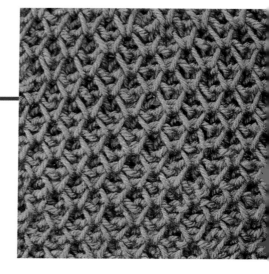

NOVEMBER
13

Braided Openwork

Multiple of 2
Row 1: Purl.
Row 2 (right side): K1, *sl 1, K1, psso, M1; rep from * to last st, K1.
Row 3: Purl.
Row 4: K1, *M1, K2tog; rep from * to last st, K1.
Rep these 4 rows.

FEBRUARY
12

Spiral Pattern

Multiple of 7

Row 1 (right side): P2, K4, *P3, K4; rep from * to last st, P1.

Row 2: K1, P3, *K4, P3; rep from * to last 3 sts, K3.

Row 3: P1, K1, P2, *K2, P2, K1, P2; rep from * to last 3 sts, K2, P1.

Row 4: K1, P1, K2, P2, *K2, P1, K2, P2; rep from * to last st, K1.

Row 5: P1, K3, *P4, K3; rep from * to last 3 sts, P3.

Row 6: K2, P4, *K3, P4; rep from * to last st, K1.

Row 7: P1, K5, *P2, K5; rep from * to last st, P1.

Row 8: K1, P5, *K2, P5; rep from * to last st, K1.

Rep these 8 rows.

NOVEMBER
12

Cellular Stitch

Multiple of 4 + 2

Row 1 (right side): K1, YO, sl 1, K2tog, psso, *YO, K1, YO, sl 1, K2tog, psso; rep from * to last 2 sts, YO, K1, YO, K1.

Row 2: Purl.

Row 3: K1, YO, K2tog, *YO, sl 1, K2tog, psso, YO, K1; rep from * to last 4 sts, YO, sl 1, K2tog, psso, K1.

Row 4: Purl.

Rep these 4 rows.

FEBRUARY
13

Lizard Lattice

Multiple of 6 + 3
Row 1 (right side): Knit.
Row 2: Purl.
Rows 3 and 4: Rep Rows 1 and 2.
Row 5: P3, *K3, P3; rep from * to end.
Row 6: Purl.
Rows 7–9: Rep Rows 5 and 6, then rep Row 5 again.
Row 10: Purl.
Row 11: Knit.
Rows 12 and 13: Rep Rows 10 and 11.
Row 14: P3, *K3, P3; rep from * to end.
Row 15: Knit.
Rows 16–18: Rep Rows 14 and 15, then rep Row 14 again.
Rep these 18 rows.

NOVEMBER
11

Oblique Openwork

Multiple of 2

Row 1 (right side): K1, P1, *YO, K1, P1; rep from * to end.

Row 2: *K1, P2tog, YO; rep from * to last 2 sts, K1, P1.

Row 3: K1, P1, *YO, K2tog, P1; rep from * to end.

Row 4: Rep from Row 2.

FEBRUARY
14

Lacy Openwork

Multiple of 4 + 1
Row 1 (right side): K1, *YO, P3tog, YO, K1; rep from * to end.
Row 2: P2tog, YO, K1, YO, *P3tog, YO, K1, YO; rep from * to last 2 sts, P2tog.
Rep these 2 rows.

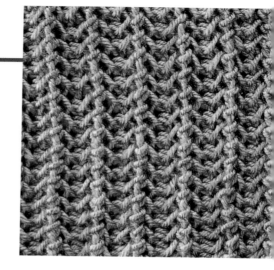

NOVEMBER
10

Houndstooth Pattern

Multiple of 3

Cast on in color A.

Row 1 (right side): Using color A, K1, *sl 1, K2; rep from * to last 2 sts, sl 1, K1.

Row 2: Using color A, purl.

Row 3: Using color B, *sl 1, K2; rep from * to end.

Row 4: Using color B, purl.

Rep these 4 rows.

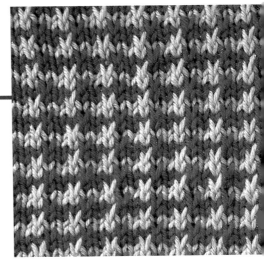

FEBRUARY
15

Simple Garter-Stitch Lace

Multiple of 4 + 2
Row 1: K2, *YO, P2tog, K2; rep from * to end.
Rep this row.

NOVEMBER
9

Trinity Stitch

Multiple of 4 + 2

Row 1 (wrong side): K1, *(K1, P1, K1) into next st, P3tog; rep from * to last st, K1.

Row 2: Purl.

Row 3: K1, *P3tog, (K1, P1, K1) into next st; rep from * to last st, K1.

Row 4: Purl.

Rep these 4 rows.

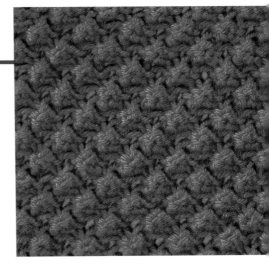

FEBRUARY
16

Purse Stitch

Multiple of 2
Row 1: P1, *YO, P2tog; rep from * to last st, P1.
Rep this row.

NOVEMBER
8

Horizontal Ridge Stitch

Multiple of 2

Row 1: Purl.

Row 2: *K1, (K1, P1, K1) into next st; rep from * to end.

Row 3: *K3, P1; rep from * to end.

Row 4: *K1, P3tog; rep from * to end.

Row 5: Purl.

Row 6: *(K1, P1, K1) into next st, K1; rep from * to end.

Row 7: *P1, K3; rep from * to end.

Row 8: *P3tog, K1; rep from * to end.

Rep these 8 rows.

FEBRUARY
17

Blanket Moss Stitch

Multiple of 2 + 1

Note: Sts should only be counted after the 2nd and 4th rows.

Row 1 (right side): Knit into front and back of each st (thus doubling the number of sts).

Row 2: K2tog, *P2tog, K2tog; rep from * to end (original number of sts restored).

Row 3: Rep Row 1.

Row 4: P2tog, *K2tog, P2tog; rep from * to end.

Rep these 4 rows.

NOVEMBER
7

Two-Color Elm-Seed Pattern

Multiple of 4 + 2

Row 1 (right side): K1, *K2 with color A, K2 with color B; rep from * to last st, K1.

Row 2: K1, *YO with color A, P2, pass YO over last 2 sts; rep from * with color B; rep from first *, alternating colors, to last st, K1.

Row 3: K1, *K2 with color B, K2 with color A; rep from * to last st, K1.

Row 4: K1, *YO with color B, P2, pass YO over last 2 sts; rep from * with color A; rep from first *, alternating colors, to last st; K1.

Rep these 4 rows.

FEBRUARY
18

Star-Stitch Pattern

Multiple of 4 + 1

Row 1 (right side): P1, *K1, P1; rep from * to end.
Row 2: K1, *MS, K1; rep from * to end.
Row 3: Rep Row 1.
Row 4: K1, P1, K1, *MS, K1; rep from * to last 2 sts, P1, K1.
Rep these 4 rows.

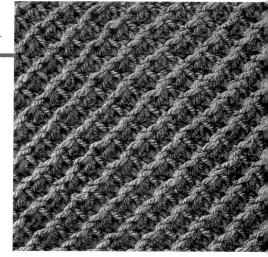

NOVEMBER
6

Ridged Slip Stitch

Multiple of 4 + 2

Row 1 (right side): K1, *K3, sl 1 wyib; rep from * to last st, K1.

Row 2: P1, *sl 1 wyif, P3; rep from * to last st, P1.

Row 3: Rep Row 1.

Row 4: Knit.

Row 5: K1, *K1, sl 1 wyib, K2; rep from * to last st, K1.

Row 6: P1, *P2, sl 1 wyif, P1; rep from * to last st, P1.

Row 7: Rep Row 5.

Row 8: Knit.

Rep these 8 rows.

FEBRUARY
19

Mock-Rib Checks

Multiple of 2
Row 1 (right side): Purl.
Row 2: *K1, K1 in st below; rep from * to last 2 sts, K2.
Rows 3–7: Rep Row 2 five more times.
Row 8: K2, *K1 in st below, K1; rep from * to end.
Rows 9–13: Rep Row 8 five more times.
Rep Rows 2–13 throughout.

NOVEMBER
5

Medallion Stitch

Multiple of 4 + 2

Row 1 (right side): K1, *sl 2 wyib, K into back of 2nd st on left-hand needle; then K first st, slipping both sts from needle tog; rep from * to last st, K1.

Row 2: K1, *sl 2 wyif, P 2nd st on left-hand needle; then P first st, slipping both sts from needle tog; rep from * to last st, K1.

Row 3: Knit.

Row 4: Purl.

Rep these 4 rows.

FEBRUARY
20

Diagonal Rib 2

Multiple of 4
Rows 1 and 2: *K2, P2; rep from * to end.
Row 3 (right side): K1, *P2, K2; rep from * to last 3 sts, P2, K1.
Row 4: P1, *K2, P2; rep from * to last 3 sts, K2, P1.
Rows 5 and 6: *P2, K2; rep from * to end.
Row 7: Rep Row 4.
Row 8: Rep Row 3.
Rep these 8 rows.

NOVEMBER
4

Tweed Mock Rib

Multiple of 2
Row 1: K1, *sl 1 purlwise, K1, YO, psso the K1 and YO; rep from * to last st, K1.
Row 2: Purl.
Rep these 2 rows.

FEBRUARY
21

Arrowhead Lace

Multiple of 10 + 1

Row 1 (right side): K1, *(YO, sl 1, K1, psso) twice, K1, (K2tog, YO) twice, K1; rep from * to end.

Row 2: Purl.

Row 3: K2, *YO, sl 1, K1, psso, YO, sl 1, K2tog, psso, YO, K2tog, YO, K3; rep from * to last 9 sts, YO, sl 1, K1, psso, YO, sl 1, K2tog, psso, YO, K2tog, YO, K2.

Row 4: Purl.

Rep these 4 rows.

NOVEMBER
3

Diagonal Crossed Stitch

Multiple of 2

Row 1: K1, *sl 1, K1, YO, psso the K1 and YO; rep from * to last st, K1.

Row 2: Purl.

Row 3: K2, *sl 1, K1, YO, psso the K1 and YO; rep from * to end.

Row 4: Purl.

Rep these 4 rows.

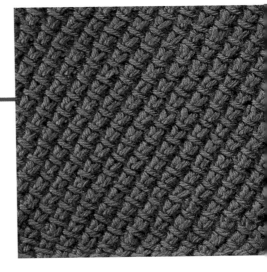

FEBRUARY
22

Climbing Leaf Pattern

Multiple of 16 + 1

Row 1 (right side): K1, *YO, K5, K2tog, K1, K2tog through back loop, K5, YO, K1; rep from * to end.

Row 2 and every even row: Purl.

Row 3: Rep Row 1.

Row 5: K1, *K2tog through back loop, K5, YO, K1, YO, K5, K2tog, K1; rep from * to end.

Row 7: Rep Row 5.

Row 8: Purl.

Rep these 8 rows.

NOVEMBER
2

Horizontal Two-One Ribs

Multiple of 3 + 1

Rows 1–4: Work 4 rows of St st, beginning with a knit row.

Row 5: K1, *P2, K1; rep from * to end.

Row 6: *K1, P2; rep from * to last st, K1.

Row 7: P1, *K2, P1; rep from * to end.

Rows 8–12: Work 5 rows of St st, beginning with a purl row.

Rep these 12 rows.

FEBRUARY
23

Lacy Zigzag

Multiple of 6 + 1

Row 1 (right side): *Sl 1, K1, psso, K2, YO, K2; rep from * to last st, K1.

Row 2: Purl.

Rows 3–6: Rep Rows 1 and 2 twice.

Row 7: K3, *YO, K2, K2tog, K2; rep from * to last 4 sts, YO, K2, K2tog.

Row 8: Purl.

Rows 9–12: Rep Rows 7 and 8 twice.

Rep these 12 rows.

NOVEMBER
1

Loop Stitch Rib

Multiple of 8 + 4

Row 1 (right side): *P4, K4 elongated sts (knit in the usual way, wrapping the yarn 3 times around the right-hand needle); rep from * to last 4 sts, P4.

Row 2: K4, *wyif, sl the 4 long sts purlwise, letting extra loops fall, K4; rep from * to end.

Row 3: *P4, sl 4 wyib, yf; rep from * to end, P4.

Row 4: Rep Row 2.

Row 5: Rep Row 1.

Rep Rows 2–5 throughout.

FEBRUARY
24

Open-Check Stitch

Multiple of 2
Row 1 (right side): Purl.
Row 2: Knit.
Row 3: K2, *sl 1, K1; rep from * to end.
Row 4: *K1, sl 1 wyif; rep from * to last 2 sts, K2.
Row 5: K1, *YO, K2tog; rep from * to last st, K1.
Row 6: Purl.
Rep these 6 rows.

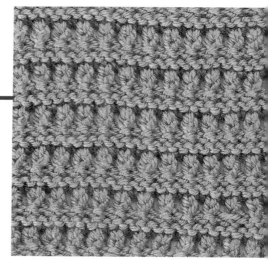

OCTOBER
31

Alternating Bobble Stitch

Multiple of 6 + 2

Row 1 and every odd row (right side): Knit.
Row 2: Purl.
Row 4: P1, *P4, make bobble: P2 (turn, sl 1 wyib, K1, turn, sl 1 wyif, P1) 3 times; rep from * to last st, P1.
Row 6: Purl.
Row 8: P1, *make bobble as before, P4; rep from * to last st, P1.
Rep these 8 rows.

FEBRUARY
25

Horizontal Herringbone

Multiple of 2

Row 1 (right side): K1, *sl 1, K1, psso but instead of dropping slipped st from left-hand needle, knit into back of it; rep from * to last st, K1.

Row 2: *P2tog, then purl first st again, slipping both sts off needle tog; rep from * to end.

Rep these 2 rows.

OCTOBER
30

Garter-Stitch Chevron

Multiple of 11

Rows 1–5: Using color A, knit.

Row 6 (right side): Using color B, *K2tog, K2, knit into front and back of next 2 sts, K3, sl 1, K1, psso; rep from * to end.

Row 7: Using color B, purl.

Rows 8–12: Rep Rows 6 and 7 twice. Work Row 6 again, using color A instead of color B.

Rep these 12 rows.

FEBRUARY
26

Herringbone

Multiple of 7 + 1

Row 1: Purl.

Row 2 (right side): *K2tog, K2, K1 through back loop of st below, then knit st above, K2; rep from * to last st, K1.

Row 3: Purl.

Row 4: K3, K1 through back loop of st below, then knit st above, K2, K2tog, *K2, K1 through back loop of st below, then knit st above, K2, K2tog; rep from * to end. Rep these 4 rows.

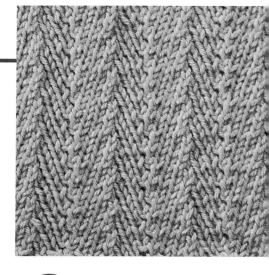

OCTOBER
29

Bicolor Tweed Stitch

Multiple of 4 + 3

Foundation row: With color A, purl.

Row 1 (right side): With color B, K1, *sl 1 wyif, K3; rep from * to last 2 sts, sl 1 wyif, K1.

Row 2: With color B, K1, sl 1 wyif, *P3, sl 1 wyif; rep from * to last st, K1.

Row 3: With color A, K1, *K2, sl 1 wyif, K1; rep from * to last 2 sts, K2.

Row 4: With color A, K1, P2, *sl 1 wyif, P3; rep from * to last 4 sts, sl 1 wyif, P2, K1.

Rep these 4 rows.

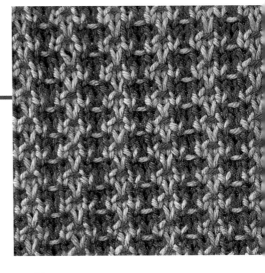

FEBRUARY
27

Open-Weave Panel

Worked over 11 sts on a background of St st

Row 1 (right side): P2, sl 1 wyib, K1, psso, YO, K3, YO, K2tog, P2.

Row 2: K2, P7, K2.

Row 3: P2, K2, YO, sl 1, K2tog, psso, YO, K2, P2.

Row 4: K2, P7, K2.

Rep these 4 rows.

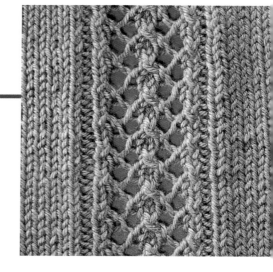

OCTOBER
28

Piqué Check Stitch

Multiple of 6

Rows 1–6: Work 6 rows of St st, beginning with a knit row.

Row 7: *K3, P3; rep from * to end.

Row 8: Purl.

Row 9: Rep Row 7.

Row 10: Purl.

Row 11: Rep Row 7.

Rows 12–18: Work 7 rows of St st, beginning with a purl row.

Row 19: *P3, K3; rep from * to end.

Row 20: Purl.

Row 21: Rep Row 19.

Row 22: Purl.

Row 23: Rep Row 19.

Row 24: Purl.

Rep these 24 rows.

FEBRUARY
28

Fan Lace Panel

Worked over 11 sts on a background of St st

Row 1 (right side): Sl 1, K1, psso, K next 3 sts through back loop, YO, K1, YO, K next 3 sts through back loop, K2tog.

Row 2 and every even row: Purl.

Row 3: Sl 1, K1, psso, K next 2 sts through back loop, YO, K1, YO, sl 1, K1, psso, YO, K next 2 sts through back loop, K2tog.

Row 5: Sl 1, K1, psso, K1 through back loop, YO, K1, (YO, sl 1, K1, psso) twice, YO, K1 through back loop, K2tog.

Row 7: Sl 1, K1, psso, YO, K1, (YO, sl 1, K1, psso) 3 times, YO, K2tog.

Row 8: Rep Row 2.

Rep these 8 rows.

OCTOBER
27

Rectangular Checks

Multiple of 6

Row 1 and every odd row (right side): Knit.

Rows 2, 4, 6, 8, 10, and 12: *K3, P3; rep from * to end.

Rows 14, 16, 18, 20, 22, and 24: *P3, K3; rep from * to end.

Rep these 24 rows.

FEBRUARY
29 (leap year)

Lace Rib Panel

Worked over 7 sts on a background of reverse St st

Row 1 (right side): P1, YO, sl 1, K1, psso, K1, K2tog, YO, P1.

Row 2: K1, P5, K1.

Row 3: P1, K1, YO, sl 1, K2tog, psso, YO, K1, P1.

Row 4: K1, P5, K1.

Rep these 4 rows.

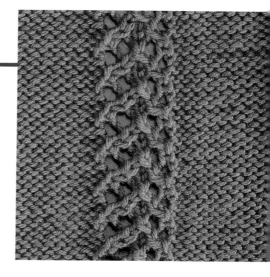

OCTOBER
26

Garter Stitch

Knit every row.

Arch Lace Panel

Worked over 11 sts on a background of St st

Row 1 (right side): K1, YO, K2tog, K5, sl 1, K1, psso, YO, K1.

Row 2 and every even row: Purl.

Row 3: Rep Row 1.

Row 5: Rep Row 1.

Row 7: K1, YO, K3, sl 1, K2tog, psso, K3, YO, K1.

Row 9: K2, YO, K2, sl 1, K2tog, psso, K2, YO, K2.

Row 11: K3, YO, K1, sl 1, K2tog, psso, K1, YO, K3.

Row 13: K4, YO, sl 1, K2tog, psso, YO, K4.

Row 14: Rep Row 2.

Rep these 14 rows.

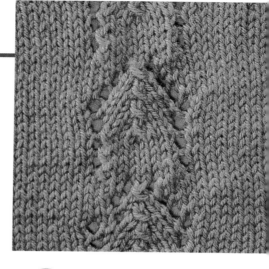

OCTOBER
25

Stockinette Stitch

Row 1 (right side): Knit.
Row 2: Purl.
Rep these 2 rows.

Foaming Waves

Multiple of 12 + 1

Rows 1–4: Knit.

Row 5 (right side): K1, *K2tog twice, (YO, K1) 3 times, YO, (sl 1, K1, psso) twice, K1; rep from * to end.

Row 6: Purl.

Rows 7–12: Rep Rows 5 and 6 three more times.

Rep these 12 rows.

OCTOBER
24

Reverse Stockinette Stitch

Row 1 (right side): Purl.
Row 2: Knit.
Rep these 2 rows.

MARCH
3

Medallion Rib

Multiple of 8 + 4

Row 1 (right side): P4, *sl 2 wyib, cross 2 back, P4; rep from * to end.

Row 2: K4, *sl 2 wyif, purl 2nd st on left-hand needle, then first st, slipping both sts from needle tog, K4; rep from * to end.

Row 3: Knit.

Row 4: Purl.

Rep these 4 rows.

OCTOBER
23

Crossed Stockinette Stitch

Row 1 (right side): Knit, working into the back of each st.
Row 2: Purl.
Rep these 2 rows.

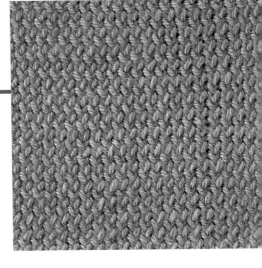

MARCH
4

Woven Rib

Multiple of 6 + 3

Row 1 (right side): P3, *sl 1 wyif, K1, sl 1 wyif, P3; rep from * to end.

Row 2: K3, *P3, K3; rep from * to end.

Row 3: *P3, K1, sl 1 wyif, K1; rep from * to last 3 sts, P3.

Row 4: Rep Row 2.

Rep these 4 rows.

OCTOBER
22

Seed Stitch 1

Odd number of stitches: Multiple of 2 + 1
Row 1: K1 *P1, K1; rep from * to end.
Rep this row.

Even number of stitches: Multiple of 2
Row 1: *K1, P1; rep from * to end.
Row 2: *P1, K1; rep from * to end.
Rep these 2 rows.

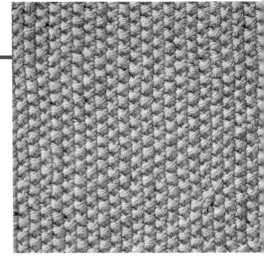

MARCH
5

Little Cable Fabric

Multiple of 4 + 1

Row 1 (right side): K1, *sl 1, K3; rep from * to end.
Row 2: *P3, sl 1; rep from * to last st, P1.
Row 3: K1, *cable 3 left, K1; rep from * to end.
Row 4: Purl.
Row 5: K5, *sl 1, K3; rep from * to end.
Row 6: *P3, sl 1; rep from * to last 5 sts, P5.
Row 7: K3, *cable 3 right, K1; rep from * to last 2 sts, K2.
Row 8: Purl.
Rep these 8 rows.

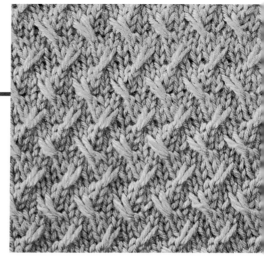

OCTOBER
21

Moss Stitch

Even number of stitches
Rows 1 and 2: *K1, P1; rep from * to end.
Rows 3 and 4: *P1, K1; rep from * to end.
Rep these 4 rows.

MARCH
6

Double Woven Stitch

Multiple of 4

Row 1 (right side): K3, *sl 2 wyif, K2; rep from * to last st, K1.

Row 2: Purl.

Row 3: K1, *sl 2 wyif, K2; rep from * to last 3 sts, sl 2 wyif, K1.

Row 4: Purl.

Rep these 4 rows.

OCTOBER
20

Box Stitch

Multiple of 4 + 2
Row 1: K2, *P2, K2; rep from * to end.
Row 2: P2, *K2, P2; rep from * to end.
Row 3: Rep Row 2.
Row 4: Rep Row 1.
Rep these 4 rows.

MARCH
7

Diamond Drops

Multiple of 4
Row 1 (right side): Knit.
Row 2: P1, *YO, P2, pass YO over purl sts, P2; rep from * to last 3 sts, YO, P2, pass YO over purl sts, P1.
Row 3: Knit.
Row 4: P3, *YO, P2, pass YO over purl sts, P2; rep from * to last st, P1.
Rep these 4 rows.

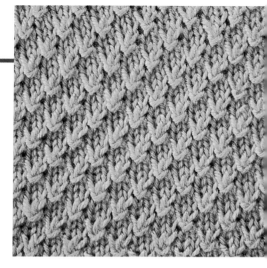

OCTOBER
19

Fleck Stitch

Multiple of 2 + 1
Row 1 (right side): Knit.
Row 2: Purl.
Row 3: K1, *P1, K1; rep from * to end.
Row 4: Purl.
Rep these 4 rows.

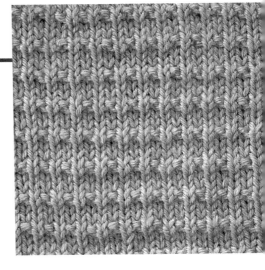

MARCH
8

Half Brioche Stitch

Multiple of 2 + 1

Row 1: Purl.

Row 2 (right side): K1, *K1 in st below, K1; rep from * to end.

Row 3: Purl.

Row 4: K1 in st below, *K1, K1 in st below; rep from * to end.

Rep these 4 rows.

OCTOBER
18

Double Fleck Stitch

Multiple of 6 + 4
Row 1 (right side): Knit.
Row 2: P4, *K2, P4; rep from * to end.
Row 3: Knit.
Row 4: P1, *K2, P4; rep from * to last 3 sts, K2, P1.
Rep these 4 rows.

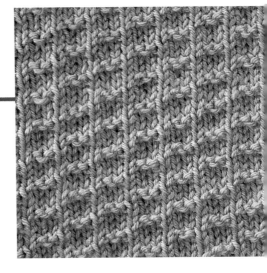

MARCH
9

Double Lace Rib

Multiple of 6 + 2

Row 1 (right side): K2, *P1, YO, K2tog through back loop, P1, K2; rep from * to end.

Row 2: P2, *K1, P2; rep from * to end.

Row 3: K2, *P1, K2tog, yfrn, P1, K2; rep from * to end.

Row 4: Rep Row 2.

Rep these 4 rows.

OCTOBER
17

Broken-Rib Diagonal

Multiple of 6
Row 1 (right side): *K4, P2; rep from * to end.
Row 2: *K2, P4; rep from * to end.
Row 3: Rep Row 1.
Row 4: Rep Row 2.
Row 5: K2, *P2, K4; rep from * to last 4 sts, P2, K2.
Row 6: P2, *K2, P4; rep from * to last 4 sts, K2, P2.
Row 7: Rep Row 5.
Row 8: Rep Row 6.
Row 9: *P2, K4; rep from * to end.
Row 10: *P4, K2; rep from * to end.
Row 11: Rep Row 9.
Row 12: Rep Row 10.
Rep these 12 rows.

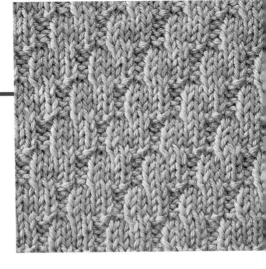

MARCH
10

Ridged Lace 2

Multiple of 2
Row 1 (right side): K1, *YO, K2tog through back loop;
rep from * to last st, K1.
Row 2: P1, *YO, P2tog; rep from * to last st, P1.
Rep these 2 rows.

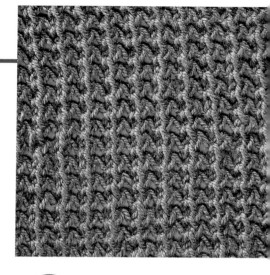

OCTOBER
16

Mock-Cable Rib

Multiple of 7 + 2

Row 1 (right side): P2, *cross 2 back, K3, P2; rep from * to end.

Row 2: K2, *P5, K2; rep from * to end.

Row 3: P2, *K1, cross 2 back, K2, P2; rep from * to end.

Row 4: Rep Row 2.

Row 5: P2, *K2, cross 2 back, K1, P2; rep from * to end.

Row 6: Rep Row 2.

Row 7: P2, *K3, cross 2 back, P2; rep from * to end.

Row 8: K2, *P5, K2; rep from * to end.

Rep these 8 rows.

MARCH
11

Scallop Pattern

Multiple of 13 + 2

Row 1 (right side): K1, *sl 1, K1, psso, K9, K2tog; rep from * to last st, K1.

Row 2: Purl.

Row 3: K1, *sl 1, K1, psso, K7, K2tog; rep from * to last st, K1.

Row 4: Purl.

Row 5: K1, *sl 1, K1, psso, YO, (K1, YO) 5 times, K2tog; rep from * to last st, K1.

Row 6: Knit.

Rep these 6 rows.

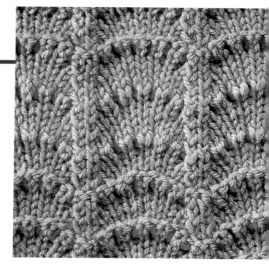

OCTOBER
15

Lattice Stitch

Multiple of 6 + 1

Row 1 (right side): K3, *P1, K5; rep from * to last 4 sts, P1, K3.

Row 2: P2, *K1, P1, K1, P3; rep from * to last 5 sts, K1, P1, K1, P2.

Row 3: K1, *P1, K3, P1, K1; rep from * to end.

Row 4: K1, *P5, K1; rep from * to end.

Row 5: Rep Row 3.

Row 6: Rep Row 2.

Rep these 6 rows.

MARCH
12

Chevron Rib 2

Multiple of 7 + 2

Row 1 (right side): K2, *K2tog, YO, K1, YO, sl 1, K1, psso, K2; rep from * to end.

Row 2: Purl.

Row 3: K1, * K2tog, YO, K3, YO, sl 1, K1, psso; rep from * to last st, K1.

Row 4: Purl.

Rep these 4 rows.

OCTOBER
14

Moss Panels

Multiple of 8 + 7

Row 1: K3, *P1, K3; rep from * to end.

Row 2 (right side): P3, *K1, P3; rep from * to end.

Row 3: K2, P1, K1, *(P1, K2) twice, P1, K1; rep from * to last 3 sts, P1, K2.

Row 4: P2, K1, P1, *(K1, P2) twice, K1, P1; rep from * to last 3 sts, K1, P2.

Row 5: K1, *P1, K1; rep from * to end.

Row 6: P1, *K1, P1; rep from * to end.

Row 7: Rep Row 3.

Row 8: Rep Row 4.

Row 9: Rep Row 1.

Row 10: Rep Row 2.

Rep these 10 rows.

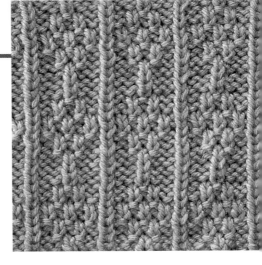

MARCH
13

Eyelet Rib

Multiple of 11 + 4

Row 1 (right side): K1, YO, P2tog, K1, *P1, K2, YO, sl 1, K1, psso, K1, P1, K1, YO, P2tog, K1; rep from * to end.

Row 2 and every even row: K1, YO, P2tog, *K2, P5, K2, YO, P2tog; rep from * to last st, K1.

Row 3: K1, YO, P2tog, K1, *P1, K1, YO, sl 1, K2tog, psso, YO, K1, P1, K1, YO, P2tog, K1; rep from * to end.

Row 5: Rep Row 1.

Row 7: K1, YO, P2tog, K1, *P1, K5, P1, K1, YO, P2tog, K1; rep from * to end.

Row 8: Rep Row 2.

Rep these 8 rows.

OCTOBER
13

Broken Rib

Multiple of 2 + 1
Row 1 (right side): Knit.
Row 2: P1, *K1, P1; rep from * to end.
Rep these 2 rows.

MARCH
14

Large Eyelet Rib

Multiple of 6 + 2
Row 1 (right side): *P2, K2tog, YO twice, sl 1, K1, psso; rep from * to last 2 sts, P2.
Row 2: K2, *P1, K1, P2, K2; rep from * to end.
Row 3: *P2, K4; rep from * to last 2 sts, P2.
Row 4: K2, *P4, K2; rep from * to end.
Rep these 4 rows.

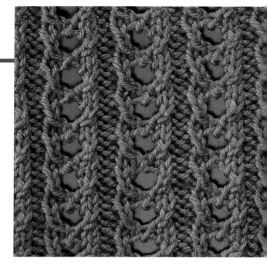

OCTOBER
12

Diagonal Rib 1

Multiple of 4

Row 1 (right side): *K2, P2; rep from * to end.
Row 2: Rep Row 1.
Row 3: K1, *P2, K2; rep from * to last 3 sts, P2, K1.
Row 4: P1, *K2, P2; rep from * to last 3 sts, K2, P1.
Row 5: *P2, K2; rep from * to end.
Row 6: Rep Row 5.
Row 7: Rep Row 4.
Row 8: Rep Row 3.
Rep these 8 rows.

MARCH
15

Eyelet Twigs

Worked over 14 sts on a background of St st

Row 1 (right side): K1, YO, K3tog, YO, K3, YO, sl 1, K2tog, psso, YO, K4.

Row 2 and every even row: Purl.

Row 3: YO, K3tog, YO, K5, YO, sl 1, K2tog, psso, YO, K3.

Row 5: K5, YO, K3tog, YO, K1, YO, sl 1, K2tog, psso, YO, K2.

Row 7: K4, YO, K3tog, YO, K3, YO, sl 1, K2tog, psso, YO, K1.

Row 9: K3, YO, K3tog, YO, K5, YO, sl 1, K2tog, psso, YO.

Row 11: K2, YO, K3tog, YO, K1, YO, sl 1, K2tog, psso, YO, K5.

Row 12: Rep Row 2.

Rep these 12 rows.

OCTOBER
11

Fisherman's Rib

Even number of sts
Row 1: Purl.
Row 2 (right side): *P1, K1 in st below; rep from * to last 2 sts, P2.
Rep Row 2 throughout.

MARCH
16

Eyelet Lace

Multiple of 6 + 2

Row 1 (right side): K1, YO, *K2tog through back loop, K2, K2tog, YO; rep from * to last st, K1.

Row 2: K1, P5, * purl into front and back of next st, P4; rep from * to last 2 sts, P1, K1.

Row 3: K2, *K2tog, YO, K2tog through back loop, K2; rep from * to end.

Row 4: K1, P2, *purl into front and back of next st, P4; rep from * to last 4 sts, purl into front and back of next st, P2, K1.

Rep these 4 rows.

OCTOBER
10

Half Fisherman's Rib

Multiple of 2 + 1

Row 1 (right side): Sl 1, knit to end.
Row 2: Sl 1, *K1 in st below, P1; rep from * to end.
Rep these 2 rows.

MARCH
17

Allover Eyelets

Multiple of 10 + 1

Row 1 (right side): Knit.

Row 2 and every even row: Purl.

Row 3: K3, * K2tog, YO, K1, YO, sl 1, K1, psso, K5; rep from * to last 8 sts, K2tog, YO, K1, YO, sl 1, K1, psso, K3.

Row 5: Knit.

Row 7: K1, *YO, sl 1, K1, psso, K5, K2tog, YO, K1; rep from * to end.

Row 8: Rep Row 2.

Rep these 8 rows.

OCTOBER
9

Little Hourglass Rib

Multiple of 4 + 2

Row 1: K2, *P2, K2; rep from * to end.

Row 2 (right side): P2, *K2tog through back loops, then knit same 2 sts tog through front loops, P2; rep from * to end.

Row 3: K2, *P1, YO, P1, K2; rep from * to end.

Row 4: P2, *sl 1 wyib, K1, psso, K1, P2; rep from * to end.

Rep these 4 rows.

MARCH
18

Rose Stitch

Multiple of 2 + 1
Row 1: K2, *P1, K1; rep from * to last st, K1.
Row 2 (right side): K1, *K1 in st below, K1; rep from * to end.
Row 3: K1, *P1, K1; rep from * to end.
Row 4: K2, *K1 in st below, K1; rep from * to last st, K1.
Rep these 4 rows.

OCTOBER
8

Dot Stitch

Multiple of 4 + 3

Row 1 (right side): K1, *P1, K3; rep from * to last 2 sts, P1, K1.

Row 2: Purl.

Row 3: *K3, P1; rep from * to last 3 sts, K3.

Row 4: Purl.

Rep these 4 rows.

MARCH
19

Twisted Check

Multiple of 4 + 2
Row 1 (right side): Knit all sts through back loops.
Row 2: Purl.
Row 3: K next 2 sts through back loop, *P2, K next 2 sts; rep from * to end.
Row 4: P2, * K2, P2; rep from * to end.
Rows 5 and 6: Rep Rows 1 and 2.
Row 7: P2, *K next 2 sts through back loop, P2; rep from * to end.
Row 8: K2, *P2, K2; rep from * to end.
Rep these 8 rows.

OCTOBER
7

Purled Ladder Stitch

Multiple of 4 + 2
Rows 1 and 2: Knit.
Row 3 (right side): P2, *K2, P2; rep from * to end.
Row 4: K2, *P2, K2; rep from * to end.
Rows 5 and 6: Knit.
Row 7: Rep Row 4.
Row 8: P2, *K2, P2; rep from * to end.
Rep these 8 rows.

MARCH
20

Spaced Knots

Multiple of 6 + 5

Rows 1–4: Work in St st, starting with a knit row.

Row 5: K5, *(K1, P1) twice into next st, K5; rep from * to end.

Row 6: P5, *sl 3, K1, pass 3 sl sts separately over last st (knot completed), P5; rep from * to end.

Rows 7–10: Work in St st, starting with a knit row.

Row 11: K2, *(K1, P1) twice into next st, K5; rep from * to last 3 sts, (K1, P1) twice into next st, K2.

Row 12: P2, *sl 3, K1, pass sl sts over as before, P5; rep from * to last 6 sts, sl 3, K1, pass sl sts over as before, P2.

Rep these 12 rows.

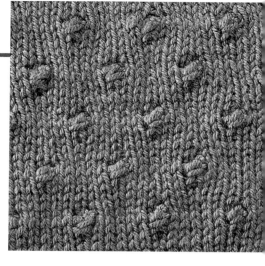

OCTOBER
6

Diamond Panels

Multiple of 8 + 1
Row 1 (right side): Knit.
Row 2: K1, *P7, K1; rep from * to end.
Row 3: K4, *P1, K7; rep from * to last 5 sts, P1, K4.
Row 4: K1, *P2, K1, P1, K1, P2, K1; rep from * to end.
Row 5: K2, *(P1, K1) twice, P1, K3; rep from * to last 7 sts, (P1, K1) twice, P1, K2.
Row 6: Rep Row 4.
Row 7: Rep Row 3.
Row 8: Rep Row 2.
Rep these 8 rows.

MARCH
21

Mock Cable on Moss Stitch

Multiple of 9 + 5

Row 1 (wrong side): (K1, P1) twice, K1, *K1 through back loop, P2, K1 through back loop, (K1, P1) twice, K1; rep from * to end.

Row 2: *(K1, P1) 3 times, K2, P1; rep from * to last 5 sts, (K1, P1) twice, K1.

Rows 3 and 4: Rep Rows 1 and 2.

Row 5: (K1, P1) twice, K1, *YO, K1, P2, K1, lift YO over last 4 sts and off needle, (K1, P1) twice, K1; rep from * to end.

Row 6: Rep Row 2.

Rep these 6 rows.

OCTOBER
5

Butterfly Lace

Multiple of 8 + 7

Row 1 (right side): K1, *K2tog, YO, K1, YO, sl 1, K1, psso, K3; rep from * to last 6 sts, K2tog, YO, K1, YO, sl 1, K1, psso, K1.

Row 2: P3, *sl 1, P7; rep from * to last 4 sts, sl 1, P3.

Row 3: Rep Row 1.

Row 4: Rep Row 2.

Row 5: K5, *K2tog, YO, K1, YO, sl 1, K1, psso, K3; rep from * to last 2 sts, K2.

Row 6: P7, *sl 1, P7; rep from * to end.

Row 7: Rep Row 5.

Row 8: Rep Row 6.

Rep these 8 rows.

MARCH
22

Zigzag Stitch

Multiple of 6
Row 1 (right side): *K3, P3; rep from * to end.
Row 2 and every even row: Purl.
Row 3: P1, *K3, P3; rep from * to last 5 sts, K3, P2.
Row 5: P2, *K3, P3; rep from * to last 4 sts, K3, P1.
Row 7: *P3, K3; rep from * to end.
Row 9: Rep Row 5.
Row 11: Rep Row 3.
Row 12: Purl.
Rep these 12 rows.

OCTOBER
4

Tile Stitch

Multiple of 6 + 4

Row 1 (right side): K4, *P2, K4; rep from * to end.
Row 2: P4, *K2, P4; rep from * to end.
Row 3: Rep Row 1.
Row 4: Rep Row 2.
Row 5: Rep Row 1.
Row 6: Rep Row 2.
Row 7: Rep Row 2.
Row 8: K4, *P2, K4; rep from * to end.
Rep these 8 rows.

March
23

Moss-Stitch Diagonal

Multiple of 8 + 3

Row 1 (right side): K4, *P1, K1, P1, K5; rep from * to last 7 sts, P1, K1, P1, K4.

Row 2: P3, *(K1, P1) twice, K1, P3; rep from * to end.

Row 3: K2, *P1, K1, P1, K5; rep from * to last st, P1.

Row 4: P1, K1, *P3, (K1, P1) twice, K1; rep from * to last st, P1.

Row 5: *P1, K1, P1, K5; rep from * to last 3 sts, P1, K1, P1.

Row 6: *(P1, K1) twice, P3, K1; rep from * to last 3 sts, P1, K1, P1.

Row 7: P1, *K5, P1, K1, P1; rep from * to last 2 sts, K2.

Row 8: (P1, K1) 3 times, *P3, (K1, P1) twice, K1; rep from * to last 5 sts, P3, K1, P1.

Rep these 8 rows.

OCTOBER
3

Ridged Rib

Multiple of 2 + 1
Rows 1 and 2: Knit.
Row 3 (right side): P1, *K1, P1; rep from * to end.
Row 4: K1, *P1, K1; rep from * to end.
Rep these 4 rows.

MARCH
24

Parallelogram Check

Multiple of 10
Row 1 (right side): *K5, P5; rep from * to end.
Row 2: K4, *P5, K5; rep from * to last 6 sts, P5, K1.
Row 3: P2, *K5, P5; rep from * to last 8 sts, K5, P3.
Row 4: K2, *P5, K5; rep from * to last 8 sts, P5, K3.
Row 5: P4, *K5, P5; rep from * to last 6 sts, K5, P1.
Row 6: *P5, K5; rep from * to end.
Rep these 6 rows.

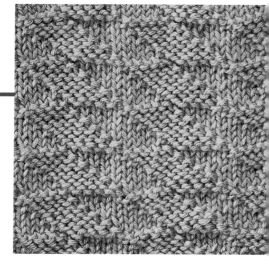

OCTOBER
2

Double-Ridged Rib

Multiple of 2 + 1
Rows 1 and 2: Knit.
Row 3 (right side): P1, *K1, P1; rep from * to end.
Row 4: K1, *P1, K1; rep from * to end.
Rows 5 and 6: Knit.
Row 7: Rep Row 4.
Row 8: P1, *K1, P1; rep from * to end.
Rep these 8 rows.

MARCH
25

Polperro Northcott

Multiple of 4 + 2

Row 1 (right side): Knit.
Rows 2 and 3: Knit.
Row 4: K2, *P2, K2; rep from * to end.
Row 5: Knit.
Rows 6–25: Rep Rows 4 and 5 ten more times.
Rows 26 and 27: Knit.
Row 28: Purl.
Rep these 28 rows.

OCTOBER
1

Interrupted Rib

Multiple of 2 + 1
Row 1 (right side): P1, *K1, P1; rep from * to end.
Row 2: K1, *P1, K1; rep from * to end.
Row 3: Purl.
Row 4: Knit.
Rep these 4 rows.

MARCH
26

Ripple Pattern

Multiple of 8 + 6

Row 1 (right side): K6, *P2, K6; rep from * to end.
Row 2: K1, *P4, K4; rep from * to last 5 sts, P4, K1.
Row 3: P2, *K2, P2; rep from * to end.
Row 4: P1, *K4, P4; rep from * to last 5 sts, K4, P1.
Row 5: K2, *P2, K6; rep from * to last 4 sts, P2, K2.
Row 6: P6, *K2, P6; rep from * to end.
Row 7: Rep Row 4.
Row 8: K2, *P2, K2; rep from * to end.
Row 9: Rep Row 2.
Row 10: P2, *K2, P6; rep from * to last 4 sts, K2, P2.
Rep these 10 rows.

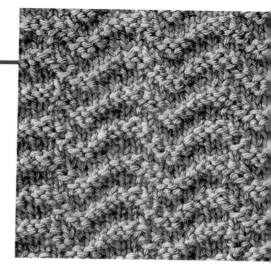

SEPTEMBER
30

Steps

Multiple of 8 + 2

Row 1 (right side): *K4, P4; rep from * to last 2 sts, K2.
Row 2: P2, *K4, P4; rep from * to end.
Row 3: Rep Row 1.
Row 4: Rep Row 2.
Row 5: K2, *P4, K4; rep from * to end.
Row 6: *P4, K4; rep from * to last 2 sts, P2.
Row 7: Rep Row 5.
Row 8: Rep Row 6.
Row 9: Rep Row 6.
Row 10: Rep Row 5.
Row 11: Rep Row 6.
Row 12: Rep Row 5.
Row 13: Rep Row 2
Row 14: Rep Row 1.
Row 15: Rep Row 2.
Row 16: Rep Row 1.
Rep these 16 rows.

MARCH
27

Moss-Stitch Parallelograms

Multiple of 10

Row 1 (right side): *K5, (P1, K1) twice, P1; rep from * to end.

Row 2: (P1, K1) 3 times, *P5, (K1, P1) twice, K1; rep from * to last 4 sts, P4.

Row 3: K3, *(P1, K1) twice, P1, K5; rep from * to last 7 sts, (P1, K1) twice, P1, K2.

Row 4: P3, *(K1, P1) twice, K1, P5; rep from * to last 7 sts, (K1, P1) twice, K1, P2.

Row 5: (K1, P1) 3 times, *K5, (P1, K1) twice, P1; rep from * to last 4 sts, K4.

Row 6: Purl.

Rep these 6 rows.

SEPTEMBER
29

Garter-Stitch Steps

Multiple of 8
Row 1 and every odd row (right side): Knit.
Row 2: *K4, P4; rep from * to end.
Row 4: Rep Row 2.
Row 6: K2, *P4, K4; rep from * to last 6 sts, P4, K2.
Row 8: Rep Row 6.
Row 10: *P4, K4; rep from * to end.
Row 12: Rep Row 10.
Row 14: P2, *K4, P4; rep from * to last 6 sts, K4, P2.
Row 16: Rep Row 14.
Rep these 16 rows.

MARCH
28

Plain Diamonds

Multiple of 9

Row 1 (right side): K4, *P1, K8; rep from * to last 5 sts, P1, K4.

Row 2: P3, *K3, P6; rep from * to last 6 sts, K3, P3.

Row 3: K2, *P5, K4; rep from * to last 7 sts, P5, K2.

Row 4: P1, *K7, P2; rep from * to last 8 sts, K7, P1.

Row 5: Purl.

Row 6: Rep Row 4.

Row 7: Rep Row 3.

Row 8: Rep Row 2.

Rep these 8 rows.

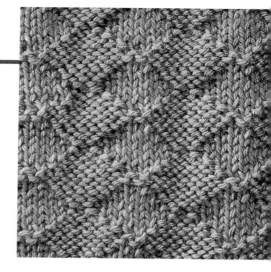

SEPTEMBER
28

Diagonal Checks

Multiple of 5
Row 1 (right side): *P1, K4; rep from * to end.
Row 2: *P3, K2; rep from * to end.
Row 3: Rep Row 2.
Row 4: Rep Row 1.
Row 5: *K1, P4; rep from * to end.
Row 6: *K3, P2; rep from * to end.
Row 7: Rep Row 6.
Row 8: Rep Row 5.
Rep these 8 rows.

MARCH
29

Chevron Stripes

Multiple of 18 + 9
Row 1 (right side): P4, K1, P4, *K4, P1, K4, P4, K1, P4;
rep from * to end.
Row 2: K3, *P3, K3; rep from * to end.
Row 3: P2, K5, P2, *K2, P5, K2, P2, K5, P2; rep from
* to end.
Row 4: K1, P7, K1, *P1, K7, P1, K1, P7, K1; rep from *
to end.
Row 5: K4, P1, K4, *P4, K1, P4, K4, P1, K4; rep from
* to end.
Row 6: P3, *K3, P3; rep from * to end.
Row 7: K2, P5, K2, *P2, K5, P2, K2, P5, K2; rep from
* to end.
Row 8: P1, K7, P1, *K1, P7, K1, P1, K7, P1; rep from *
to end.
Rep these 8 rows.

SEPTEMBER
27

Stockinette Ridge

Multiple of 2
Row 1 (right side): Knit.
Row 2: P1, *K2tog; rep from * to last st, P1.
Row 3: K1, *knit into front and back of next st; rep from * to last st, K1.
Row 4: Purl.
Rep these 4 rows.

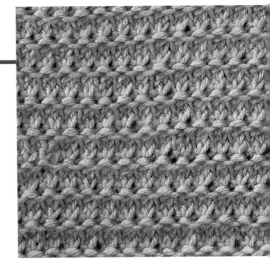

MARCH
30

Moss-Stitch Panes

Multiple of 10 + 3

Row 1 (right side): P1, *K1, P1; rep from * to end.

Row 2: P1, *K1, P1; rep from * to end.

Row 3: P1, K1, P1, *K7, P1, K1, P1; rep from * to end.

Row 4: P1, K1, P9, *K1, P9; rep from * to last 2 sts, K1, P1.

Rows 5–10: Rep Rows 3 and 4 three more times. Rep these 10 rows.

Ridged Knot Stitch

Multiple of 3 + 2
Row 1 (right side): Knit.
Row 2: K1, *MK; rep from * to last st, K1.
Rows 3 and 4: Knit.
Rep these 4 rows.

MARCH
31

Moss-Stitch Triangles

Multiple of 8

Row 1 (right side): *P1, K7; rep from * to end.
Row 2: P6, *K1, P7; rep from * to last 2 sts, K1, P1.
Row 3: *P1, K1, P1, K5; rep from * to end.
Row 4: P4, *K1, P1, K1, P5; rep from * to last 4 sts, (K1, P1) twice.
Row 5: *(P1, K1) twice, P1, K3; rep from * to end.
Row 6: P2, *(K1, P1) twice, K1, P3; rep from * to last 6 sts, (K1, P1) 3 times.
Row 7: *P1, K1; rep from * to end.
Row 8: Rep Row 6.
Row 9: Rep Row 5.
Row 10: Rep Row 4.
Row 11: Rep Row 3.
Row 12: Rep Row 2.
Rep these 12 rows.

SEPTEMBER
25

Bramble Stitch

Multiple of 4 + 2
Row 1 (right side): Purl.
Row 2: K1, *(K1, P1, K1) into next st, P3tog; rep from
* to last st, K1.
Row 3: Purl.
Row 4: K1, *P3tog, (K1, P1, K1) into next st; rep from
* to last st, K1.
Rep these 4 rows.

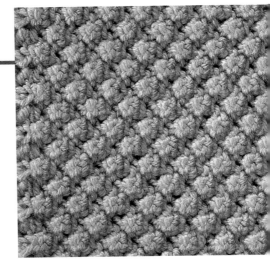

APRIL
1

Triangle Rib

Multiple of 8
Row 1 (right side): *P2, K6; rep from * to end.
Row 2: *P6, K2; rep from * to end.
Row 3: *P3, K5; rep from * to end.
Row 4: *P4, K4; rep from * to end.
Row 5: *P5, K3; rep from * to end.
Row 6: *P2, K6; rep from * to end.
Row 7: *P7, K1; rep from * to end.
Row 8: *P2, K6; rep from * to end.
Row 9: Rep Row 5.
Row 10: Rep Row 4.
Row 11: Rep Row 3.
Row 12: Rep Row 2.
Rep these 12 rows.

SEPTEMBER
24

Alternating Triangles

Multiple of 5
Row 1 (right side): *P1, K4; rep from * to end.
Rows 2 and 3: *P3, K2; rep from * to end.
Row 4: Rep Row 1.
Row 5: *K4, P1; rep from * to end.
Rows 6 and 7: *K2, P3; rep from * to end.
Row 8: Rep Row 5.
Rep these 8 rows.

APRIL
2

Brioche Rib

Multiple of 2
Row 1: Knit.
Row 2 (right side): *K1, K1 in st below; rep from * to last 2 sts, K2.
Rep Row 2 throughout.

SEPTEMBER
23

Twisted Check Pattern

Multiple of 8 + 5

Row 1 (right side): Purl.

Row 2: K1, *P next 3 sts through back loop, K5; rep from * to last 4 sts, P next 3 sts through back loop, K1.

Row 3: P1, *K next 3 sts through back loop, P5; rep from * to last 4 sts, K next 3 sts through back loop, P1.

Row 4: Rep Row 2.

Row 5: Purl.

Row 6: Knit.

Row 7: P5, *K next 3 sts through back loop, P5; rep from * to end.

Row 8: K5, *P next 3 sts through back loop, K5; rep from * to end.

Row 9: Rep Row 7.

Row 10: Knit.

Rep these 10 rows.

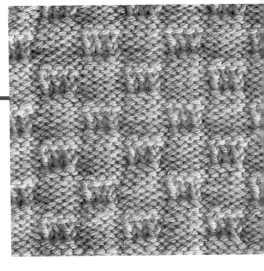

APRIL
3

Garter-Stitch Ridges

Any number of stitches
Row 1 (right side): Knit.
Row 2: Purl.
Row 3: Knit.
Row 4: Purl.
Rows 5–10: Purl.
Rep these 10 rows.

SEPTEMBER
22

Stockinette Triangles

Multiple of 5
Row 1 (right side): Knit.
Row 2: *K1, P4; rep from * to end.
Row 3: *K3, P2; rep from * to end.
Row 4: Rep Row 3.
Row 5: Rep Row 2.
Row 6: Knit.
Rep these 6 rows.

APRIL
4

Zigzag Moss Stitch

Multiple of 6 + 1

Row 1 (right side): Knit.

Row 2: Purl.

Row 3: P1, *K5, P1; rep from * to end.

Row 4: P1, *K1, P3, K1, P1; rep from * to end.

Rows 5 and 6: P1, *K1, P1; rep from * to end.

Row 7: K2, P1, K1, P1, *K3, P1, K1, P1; rep from * to last 2 sts, K2.

Row 8: P3, K1, *P5, K1; rep from * to last 3 sts, P3.

Row 9: Knit.

Row 10: Purl.

Row 11: K3, *P1, K5; rep from * to last 4 sts, P1, K3.

Row 12: P2, *K1, P1, K1, P3; rep from * to last 5 sts; K1, P1, K1, P2.

Rows 13 and 14: K1, *P1, K1; rep from * to end.

Row 15: K1, P1, *K3, P1, K1, P1; rep from * to last 5 sts, K3, P1, K1.

Row 16: K1, *P5, K1; rep from * to end.

Rep these 16 rows.

SEPTEMBER
21

Lichen Twist

Multiple of 4 + 2

Row 1 (right side): *K1 through back loop; rep from * to end.

Row 2: *P1 through back loop; rep from * to end.

Row 3: P2, *cross 2 back, P2; rep from * to end.

Row 4: K2, *P2, K2; rep from * to end.

Row 5: Rep Row 1.

Row 6: Rep Row 2.

Row 7: K2, *P2, cross 2 back; rep from * to last 4 sts, P2, K2.

Row 8: P2, *K2, P2; rep from * to end.

Rep these 8 rows.

APRIL
5

Moss-Stitch Diamonds

Multiple of 10 + 9

Row 1 (right side): K4, *P1, K9; rep from * to last 5 sts, P1, K4.

Row 2: P3, *K1, P1, K1, P7; rep from * to last 6 sts, K1, P1, K1, P3.

Row 3: K2, *(P1, K1) twice, P1, K5; rep from * to last 7 sts, (P1, K1) twice, P1, K2.

Row 4: (P1, K1) 4 times, *P3, (K1, P1) 3 times, K1; rep from * to last st, P1.

Row 5: P1, *K1, P1; rep from * to end.

Row 6: Rep Row 4.

Row 7: Rep Row 3.

Row 8: Rep Row 2.

Row 9: Rep Row 1.

Row 10: Purl.

Rep these 10 rows.

SEPTEMBER
20

Twisted Basket Weave

Multiple of 8 + 5
Row 1 (right side): P5, *cross 3, P5; rep from * to end.
Row 2: K5, *P3, K5; rep from * to end.
Row 3: Rep Row 1.
Row 4: Rep Row 2.
Row 5: P1, *cross 3, P5; rep from * to last 4 sts, cross 3, P1.
Row 6: K1, *P3, K5; rep from * to last 4 sts, P3, K1.
Row 7: Rep Row 5.
Row 8: Rep Row 6.
Rep these 8 rows.

APRIL
6

Double Signal Check

Multiple of 18 + 9

Row 1 (right side): K1, P7, K1, *P1, K7, P1, K1, P7, K1; rep from * to end.

Row 2: P2, K5, P2, *K2, P5, K2, P2, K5, P2; rep from * to end.

Row 3: K3, *P3, K3; rep from * to end.

Row 4: P4, K1, P4, *K4, P1, K4, P4, K1, P4; rep from * to end.

Row 5: P1, K7, P1, *K1, P7, K1, P1, K7, P1; rep from * to end.

Row 6: K2, P5, K2, *P2, K5, P2, K2, P5, K2; rep from * to end.

Row 7: P3, *K3, P3; rep from * to end.

Row 8: K4, P1, K4, *P4, K1, P4, K4, P1, K4; rep from * to end.

Rep these 8 rows.

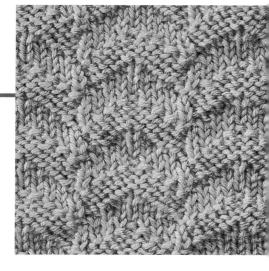

SEPTEMBER
19

Cable Fabric

Multiple of 6
Row 1 (right side): Knit.
Row 2 and every even row: Purl.
Row 3: *K2, cable 4 back; rep from * to end.
Row 5: Knit.
Row 7: *Cable 4 front, K2; rep from * to end.
Row 8: Rep Row 2.
Rep these 8 rows.

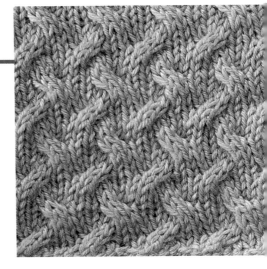

APRIL
7

Seed-Stitch Checks

Multiple of 10 + 5

Row 1 (right side): K5, *(P1, K1) twice, P1, K5; rep from * to end.

Row 2: P6, *K1, P1, K1, P7; rep from * to last 9 sts, K1, P1, K1, P6.

Row 3: Rep Row 1.

Row 4: Rep Row 2.

Row 5: Rep Row 1.

Row 6: *(K1, P1) twice, K1, P5; rep from * to last 5 sts, (K1, P1) twice, K1.

Row 7: (K1, P1) twice, *K7, P1, K1, P1; rep from * to last st, K1.

Row 8: Rep Row 6.

Row 9: Rep Row 7.

Row 10: Rep Row 6.

Rep these 10 rows.

SEPTEMBER
18

Diagonal Knot Stitch

Multiple of 3 + 1

Row 1 and every odd row (right side): Knit.
Row 2: *MK; rep from * to last st, P1.
Row 4: P2, *MK; rep from * to last 2 sts, P2.
Row 6: P1, *MK; rep from * to end.
Rep these 6 rows.

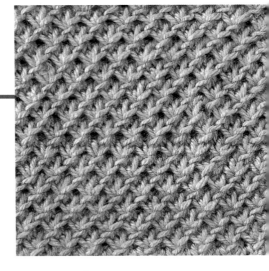

APRIL
8

Double Andalusian Stitch

Multiple of 6

Row 1 (right side): Knit.
Row 2: *K2, P4; rep from * to end.
Row 3: Knit.
Row 4: P3, *K2, P4; rep from * to last 3 sts; K2, P1.
Row 5: Knit.
Rep Rows 2–5 throughout.

SEPTEMBER
17

Slip-Stitch Rib

Multiple of 2 + 1
Row 1: Purl.
Row 2 (right side): K1, *sl 1 wyif, K1; rep from * to end.
Rep these 2 rows.

APRIL
9

Andalusian Stitch

Multiple of 2
Row 1 (right side): Knit.
Row 2: Purl.
Row 3: *K1, P1; rep from * to end.
Row 4: Purl.
Rep these 4 rows.

SEPTEMBER
16

Pillar Stitch

Multiple of 2
Row 1: Purl.
Row 2 (right side): K1, *YO, K2, pass YO over K2; rep from * to last st, K1.
Rep these 2 rows.

APRIL
10

Double Seed Stitch

Multiple of 5 + 2

Row 1 (right side): K2, *P3, K2; rep from * to end.
Row 2: Purl.
Row 3: *P3, K2; rep to last 2 sts, P2.
Row 4: Purl.
Rep these 4 rows.

SEPTEMBER
15

Garter Drop Stitch

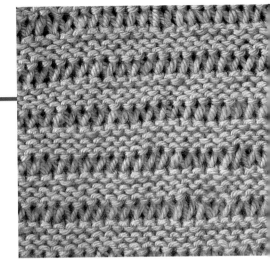

Any number of stitches

Rows 1–4: Work in garter st (knit every row).

Row 5: *K1, winding yarn twice around needle; rep from * to end.

Row 6: Knit to end, dropping the extra loops.

Rep these 6 rows.

APRIL
11

Seed Stitch 3

Multiple of 4 + 3
Row 1: P1, K1, *P3, K1; rep from * to last st, P1.
Row 2 (right side): K3, *P1, K3; rep from * to end.
Rep these 2 rows.

SEPTEMBER
14

Lattice Lace

Multiple of 7 + 2

Row 1 (right side): K3, *K2tog, YO, K5; rep from * to last 6 sts, K2tog, YO, K4.

Row 2: P2, *P2tog through back loop, YO, P1, YO, P2tog, P2; rep from * to end.

Row 3: K1, *K2tog, YO, K3, YO, sl 1, K1, psso; rep from * to last st, K1.

Row 4: Purl.

Row 5: K1, *YO, sl 1, K1, psso, K5; rep from * to last st, K1.

Row 6: *P1, YO, P2tog, P2, P2tog through back loop, YO; rep from * to last 2 sts, P2.

Row 7: *K3, YO, sl 1, K1, psso, K2tog, YO; rep from * to last 2 sts, K2.

Row 8: Purl.

Rep these 8 rows.

APRIL
12

Seed Stitch 2

Multiple of 4 + 3
Row 1 (right side): P1, K1, *P3, K1; rep from * to last st, P1.
Row 2: K3, *P1, K3; rep from * to end.
Rep these 2 rows.

SEPTEMBER
13

Lacy Checks

Multiple of 6 + 5
Row 1 (right side): K1, *YO, sl 1, K2tog, psso, YO, K3;
rep from * to last 4 sts, YO, sl 1, K2tog, psso, YO, K1.
Row 2 and every even row: Purl.
Row 3: Rep Row 1.
Row 5: Knit.
Row 7: K4, *yf, sl 1, K2tog, psso, yf, K3; rep from * to
last st, K1.
Row 9: Rep Row 7.
Row 11: Knit.
Row 12: Rep Row 2.
Rep these 12 rows.

APRIL
13

Knot Stitch

Multiple of 2 + 1

Row 1 (right side): Knit.

Row 2: K1, *P2tog without slipping sts off needle, then knit tog the same 2 sts; rep from * to end.

Row 3: Knit.

Row 4: *P2tog without slipping sts off needle, then knit tog the same 2 sts; rep from * to last st, K1.

Rep these 4 rows.

SEPTEMBER
12

Garter and Slip Stitch

Multiple of 6 + 4

Row 1 (right side): Knit.

Row 2: K1, *sl 2 wyif, K4; rep from * to last 3 sts, sl 2 wyif, K1.

Row 3: K1, *sl 2 wyib, K4; rep from * to last 3 sts, sl 2, K1.

Row 4: Rep Row 2.

Row 5: Rep Row 3.

Row 6: Rep Row 2.

Row 7: Knit.

Row 8: K4, *sl 2 wyif, K4; rep from * to end.

Row 9: K4, *sl 2 wyib, K4; rep from * to end.

Row 10: Rep Row 8.

Row 11: Rep Row 9.

Row 12: Rep Row 8.

Rep these 12 rows.

APRIL
14

Woven Stitch 2

Multiple of 2 + 1

Row 1 (right side): K1, *sl 1 wyif, K1; rep from * to end.

Row 2: Purl.

Row 3: K2, *sl 1 wyif, K1; rep from * to last st, K1.

Row 4: Purl.

Rep these 4 rows.

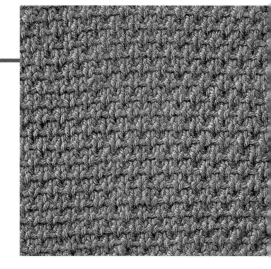

SEPTEMBER
11

Moss-Stitch Squares

Multiple of 12 + 3

Row 1 (right side): Knit.

Row 2: Purl.

Row 3: K4, *(P1, K1) 3 times, P1, K5; rep from * to last 11 sts, (P1, K1) 3 times, P1, K4.

Row 4: P3, *(K1, P1) 4 times, K1, P3; rep from * to end.

Row 5: K4, *P1, K5; rep from * to last 5 sts, P1, K4.

Row 6: P3, *K1, P7, K1, P3; rep from * to end.

Rows 7–11: Rep Rows 5 and 6 twice more; then rep Row 5 again.

Row 12: Rep Row 4.

Row 13: Rep Row 3.

Row 14: Purl.

Rep these 14 rows.

APRIL
15

Tweed Stitch

Multiple of 2 + 1
Row 1 (right side): K1, *sl 1 wyib, K1; rep from * to end.
Row 2: P2, *sl 1 wyib, P1; rep from * to last st, P1.
Rep these 2 rows.

September
10

Staggered Eyelets

Multiple of 4 + 3
Row 1: Knit.
Row 2: Purl.
Row 3 (right side): *K2, K2tog, YO; rep from * to last 3 sts, K3.
Row 4: Purl.
Row 5: Knit.
Row 6: Purl.
Row 7: *K2tog, YO, K2; rep from * to last 3 sts, K2tog, YO, K1.
Row 8: Purl.
Rep these 8 rows.

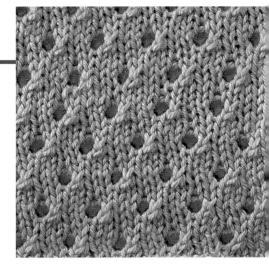

APRIL
16

Knit-Two, Purl-Two Rib

Multiple of 4
Row 1: *K2, P2; rep from * to end.
Rep this row.

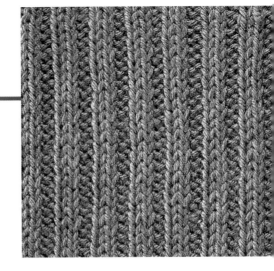

SEPTEMBER
9

Fir Cone

Multiple of 10 + 1

Row 1: Purl.

Row 2 (right side): K1, *YO, K3, sl 1, K2tog, psso, K3, YO, K1; rep from * to end.

Rows 3–8: Rep Rows 1 and 2 three more times.

Row 9: Purl.

Row 10: K2tog, *K3, YO, K1, YO, K3, sl 1, K2tog, psso; rep from * to last 9 sts, K3, YO, K1, YO, K3, sl 1, K1, psso.

Rows 11–16: Rep Rows 9 and 10 three more times. Rep these 16 rows.

APRIL
17

Knit-One, Purl-One Rib

Multiple of 2
Row 1: *K1, P1; rep from * to end.
Rep this row.

SEPTEMBER
8

Wavy Eyelet Rib

Multiple of 7 + 2

Row 1 (right side): *P2, YO, sl 1, K1, psso, K1, K2tog, YO; rep from * to last 2 sts, P2.

Row 2 and every even row: K2, *P5, K2; rep from * to end.

Row 3: Rep Row 1.

Row 5: Rep Row 1.

Row 7: *P2, K5; rep from * to last 2 sts, P2.

Row 9: *P2, K2tog, YO, K1, YO, sl 1, K1, psso; rep from * to last 2 sts, P2.

Row 11: Rep Row 9.

Row 13: Rep Row 9.

Row 15: Rep Row 7.

Row 16: Rep Row 2.

Rep these 16 rows.

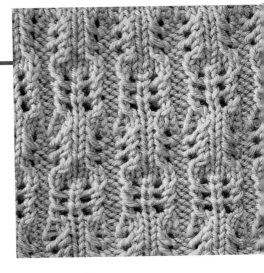

APRIL
18

Two-Stitch Rib

Multiple of 4 + 2
Row 1: K2, *P2, K2; rep from * to end.
Rep this row.

SEPTEMBER
7

Bluebell Rib

Multiple of 5 + 2

Row 1 (right side): P2, *K3, P2; rep from * to end.

Row 2: K2, *P3, K2; rep from * to end.

Row 3: Rep Row 1.

Row 4: Rep Row 2.

Row 5: P2, *YO, sl 1, K2tog, psso, YO, P2; rep from * to end.

Row 6: Rep Row 2.

Rep these 6 rows.

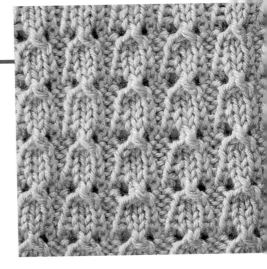

APRIL
19

Diagonal Garter Ribs

Multiple of 5 + 2
Row 1 and every odd row (right side): Knit.
Row 2: *P2, K3; rep from * to last 2 sts, P2.
Row 4: K1, *P2, K3; rep from * to last st, P1.
Row 6: K2, *P2, K3; rep from * to end.
Row 8: *K3, P2; rep from * to last 2 sts, K2.
Row 10: P1, *K3, P2; rep from * to last st, K1.
Rep these 10 rows.

SEPTEMBER
6

Granite Rib

Multiple of 8 + 2

Row 1 (right side): K2 *(cross 2 front) 3 times, K2; rep from * to end.

Row 2: Purl.

Row 3: K2, *(knit 3rd st from left-hand needle, then 2nd st, then first st, slipping all 3 sts off needle tog) twice, K2; rep from * to end.

Row 4: Purl.

Rep these 4 rows.

APRIL
20

Wavy Rib

Multiple of 6 + 2

Row 1 (right side): P2, *K4, P2; rep from * to end.
Row 2: K2, *P4, K2; rep from * to end.
Row 3: Rep Row 1.
Row 4: Rep Row 2.
Row 5: K3, P2, *K4, P2; rep from * to last 3 sts, K3.
Row 6: P3, K2, *P4, K2; rep from * to last 3 sts, P3.
Row 7: Rep Row 5.
Row 8: Rep Row 6.
Rep these 8 rows.

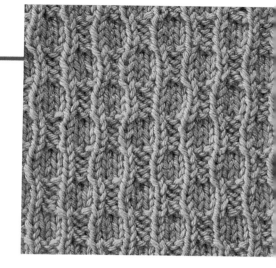

SEPTEMBER
5

Ripple Rib

Multiple of 3 + 1
Row 1: K1, *P2, K1; rep from * to end.
Row 2 (right side): P1, *cross 2 front, P1; rep from *
to end.
Row 3: Rep Row 1.
Row 4: P1, *cross 2 back, P1; rep from * to end.
Rep these 4 rows.

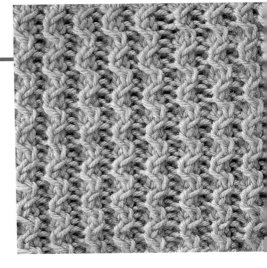

April
21

Small Basket Stitch

Multiple of 10 + 5

Row 1 (wrong side): (K1, P1) twice, *K7, P1, K1, P1; rep from * to last st, K1.

Row 2: P1, (K1, P1) twice, *K5, (P1, K1) twice, P1; rep from * to end.

Row 3: Rep Row 1.

Row 4: Rep Row 2.

Row 5: K6, *P1, K1, P1, K7; rep from * to last 9 sts, P1, K1, P1, K6.

Row 6: *K5, (P1, K1) twice, P1; rep from * to last 5 sts, K5.

Row 7: Rep Row 5.

Row 8: Rep Row 6.

Rep these 8 rows.

SEPTEMBER
4

Square Rib

Multiple of 2 + 1

Row 1 (right side): K2, P1, *K1, P1; rep from * to last 2 sts, K2.

Row 2: K1, *P1, K1; rep from * to end.

Row 3: Rep Row 1.

Row 4: K1, P1, *yb, insert needle through center of st 2 rows below next st on needle and knit this in the usual way, slipping st above it off needle at the same time, P1; rep from * to last st, K1.

Rep these 4 rows.

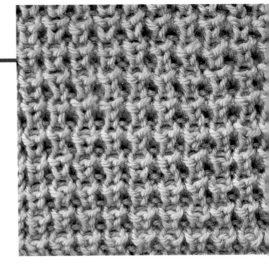

APRIL
22

Basket Weave 2

Multiple of 8 + 3
Row 1 (right side): Knit.
Row 2: K4, P3, *K5, P3; rep from * to last 4 sts, K4.
Row 3: P4, K3, *P5, K3; rep from * to last 4 sts, P4.
Row 4: Rep Row 2.
Row 5: Knit.
Row 6: P3, *K5, P3; rep from * to end.
Row 7: K3, *P5, K3; rep from * to end.
Row 8: Rep Row 6.
Rep these 8 rows.

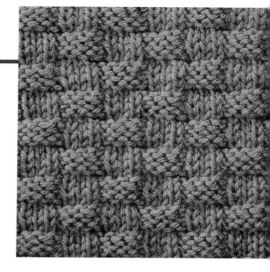

SEPTEMBER
3

Faggoted Rib

Multiple of 4 + 2
Row 1 (right side): K3, *YO, sl 1, K1, psso, K2; rep from * to last 3 sts, YO, sl 1, K1, psso, K1.
Row 2: P3, *YO, P2tog, P2; rep from * to last 3 sts, YO, P2tog, P1.
Rep these 2 rows.

APRIL
23

Basket Weave 1

Multiple of 4 + 3
Rows 1 and 3 (right side): Knit.
Row 2: *K3, P1; rep from * to last 3 sts, K3.
Row 4: K1, *P1, K3; rep from * to last 2 sts, P1, K1.
Rep these 4 rows.

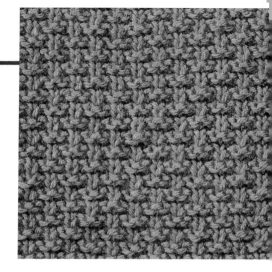

SEPTEMBER
2

Basket Weave Rib

Multiple of 15 + 8
Row 1 (right side): *P3, K2, P3, K1, (cross 2 front) 3 times; rep from * to last 8 sts, P3, K2, P3.
Row 2: *K3, cross 2 purl, K3, P1, (cross 2 purl) 3 times; rep from * to last 8 sts, K3, cross 2 purl, K3.
Rep these 2 rows.

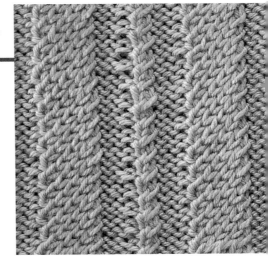

APRIL
24

Waffle Stitch

Multiple of 3 + 1
Row 1 (right side): P1, *K2, P1; rep from * to end.
Row 2: K1, *P2, K1; rep from * to end.
Row 3: Rep Row 1.
Row 4: Knit.
Rep these 4 rows.

SEPTEMBER
1

Chain-Stitch Rib

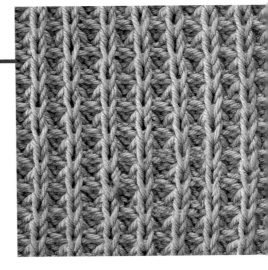

Multiple of 3 + 2

Row 1: K2, *P1, K2; rep from * to end.

Row 2 (right side): P2, *K1, P2; rep from * to end.

Row 3: Rep Row 1.

Row 4: P2, *yb, insert needle through center of st 3 rows below next st on needle and knit this in the usual way, slipping st above it off needle at the same time; P2; rep from * to end.

Rep these 4 rows.

APRIL
25

Chevron
and Feather

Multiple of 13 + 1
Row 1 (right side): *K1, YO, K4, K2tog, sl 1, K1, psso, K4, YO; rep from * to last st, K1.
Row 2: Purl.
Rep these 2 rows.

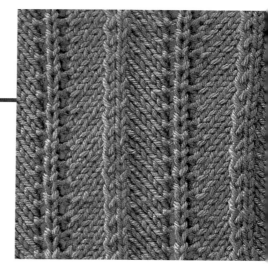

AUGUST
31

Linked Ribs

Multiple of 8 + 4

Row 1 (right side): P4, *K1, P2, K1, P4; rep from * to end.

Row 2: K4, *P1, K2, P1, K4; rep from * to end.

Row 3: Rep Row 1.

Row 4: Rep Row 2.

Row 5: P4, *cross 2 left, cross 2 right, P4; rep from * to end.

Row 6: K4, *P4, K4; rep from * to end.

Rep these 6 rows.

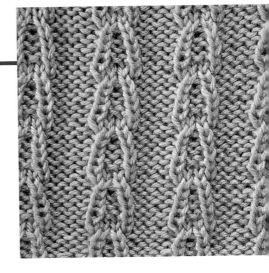

APRIL
26

Giant Cable

Worked over 12 sts on a background of reverse St st

Row 1 (right side): Knit.

Row 2: Purl.

Rows 3 and 4: Rep Rows 1 and 2.

Row 5: Cable 12 back.

Row 6: Purl.

Rows 7 and 8: Rep Rows 1 and 2.

Rep these 8 rows.

These instructions result in a cable that twists to the right (shown at right in photo). To twist the cable to the left (shown at left in photo), hold the cable to the front instead of the back in Row 5.

AUGUST
30

Chevron Rib 1

Multiple of 18 + 1

Row 1 (right side): P1, *K1, P2, K2, P2, K1, P1; rep from * to end.

Row 2: *K3, P2, K2, P2, K1, (P2, K2) twice; rep from * to last st, K1.

Row 3: *(P2, K2) twice, P3, K2, P2, K2, P1; rep from * to last st, P1.

Row 4: *K1, P2, K2, P2, K5, P2, K2, P2; rep from * to last st, K1.

Rep these 4 rows.

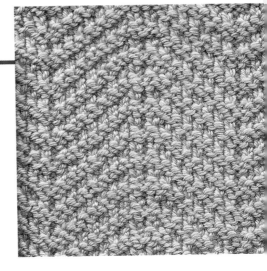

APRIL
27

Wave Cable

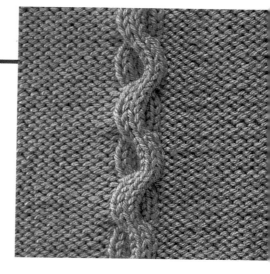

Worked over 6 sts on a background of reverse St st

Row 1 (right side): Knit.
Row 2: Purl.
Row 3: Cable 6 back.
Row 4: Purl.
Rows 5–8: Rep Rows 1 and 2 twice.
Row 9: Cable 6 front.
Row 10: Purl.
Rows 11 and 12: Rep Rows 1 and 2.
Rep these 12 rows.

AUGUST
29

Little Chevron Rib

Multiple of 10 + 1

Row 1 (right side): P1, *K1, P1, (K2, P1) twice, K1, P1; rep from * to end.

Row 2: K1, *P2, (K1, P1) twice, K1, P2, K1; rep from * to end.

Row 3: P1, *K3, P3, K3, P1; rep from * to end.

Row 4: K2, *P3, K1, P3, K3; rep from * to last 9 sts, P3, K1, P3, K2.

Rep these 4 rows.

APRIL
28

Star Stitch

Multiple of 4 + 1

Row 1 (right side): Knit.
Row 2: P1, *MS, P1; rep from * to end.
Row 3: Knit.
Row 4: P3, MS, *P1, MS; rep from * to last 3 sts, P3.

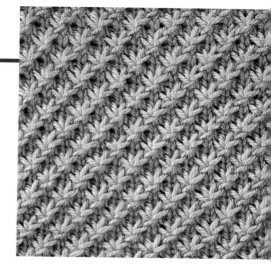

AUGUST
28

Vandyke Lace Panel 1

Worked over 17 sts on a background of St st
Row 1 (right side): *K2tog, YO, K1, YO, sl 1, K1, psso,*
K3, YO, sl 1, K1, psso, K2; rep from * to * once more.
Row 2: Purl.
Row 3: (K2tog, YO, K1, YO, sl 1, K1, psso, K1) twice,
K2tog, YO, K1, YO, sl 1, K1, psso.
Row 4: Purl.
Row 5: *K2tog, YO, K1, YO, sl 1, K1, psso,* K2tog, YO,
K3, YO, sl 1, K1, psso; rep from * to * once more.
Row 6: Purl.
Rep these 6 rows.

APRIL
29

Eyelet Lattice Insertion

Worked over 8 sts on a background of St st
Row 1 (right side): K1, (K2tog, YO) 3 times, K1.
Row 2: Purl.
Row 3: K2, (K2tog, YO) twice, K2.
Row 4: Purl.
Rep these 4 rows.

AUGUST
27

Vandyke Lace Panel 2

Worked over 9 sts on a background of St st
Row 1 (right side): K4, YO, sl 1, K1, psso, K3.
Row 2 and every even row: Purl.
Row 3: K2, K2tog, YO, K1, YO, sl 1, K1, psso, K2.
Row 5: K1, K2tog, YO, K3, YO, sl 1, K1, psso, K1.
Row 7: K2tog, YO, K5, YO, sl 1, K1, psso.
Row 8: Rep Row 2.
Rep these 8 rows.

APRIL
30

Little Shell Insertion

Worked over 7 sts on a background of St st
Row 1 (right side): Knit.
Row 2: Purl.
Row 3: K1, YO, P1, P3tog, P1, YO, K1.
Row 4: Purl.
Rep these 4 rows.

AUGUST
26

Tulip Lace

Multiple of 8 + 7

Row 1 (right side): Knit.

Row 2 and every even row: Purl.

Row 3: K3, *YO, sl 1, K1, psso, K6; rep from * to last 4 sts, YO, sl 1, K1, psso, K2.

Row 5: K1, *K2tog, YO, K1, YO, sl 1, K1, psso, K3; rep from * to last 6 sts, K2tog, YO, K1, YO, sl 1, K1, psso, K1.

Row 7: Rep Row 3.

Row 9: Knit.

Row 11: K7, *YO, sl 1, K1, psso, K6; rep from * to end.

Row 13: K5, *K2tog, YO, K1, YO, sl 1, K1, psso, K3; rep from * to last 2 sts, K2.

Row 15: Rep Row 11.

Row 16: Rep Row 2.

Rep these 16 rows.

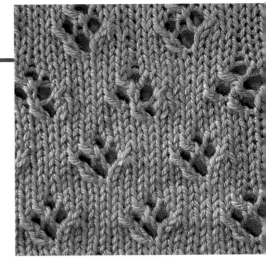

MAY
1

Branched Cable 2

Worked over 10 sts on a background of reverse St st

Row 1 (right side): P3, cable 4 front, P3.

Row 2: K3, P4, K3.

Row 3: P2, cross 3 back, cross 3 front, P2.

Row 4: K2, P6, K2.

Row 5: P1, cross 3 back, K2, cross 3 front, P1.

Row 6: K1, P8, K1.

Row 7: Cross 3 back, K4, cross 3 front.

Row 8: Purl.

Rep these 8 rows.

AUGUST
25

Fishtail Lace Panel

Worked over 11 sts on a background of St st

Row 1 (right side): P1, K1, YO, K2, sl 1, K2tog, psso, K2, YO, K1, P1.

Row 2: K1, P9, K1.

Row 3: P1, K2, YO, K1, sl 1, K2tog, psso, K1, YO, K2, P1.

Row 4: Rep Row 2.

Row 5: P1, K3, YO, sl 1, K2tog, psso, YO, K3, P1.

Row 6: Rep Row 2.

Rep these 6 rows.

MAY
2

Twisted Tree

Worked over 9 sts on a background of reverse St st

Row 1 (right side): P3, K next 3 sts through back loop, P3.

Row 2: K3, P next 3 sts through back loop, K3.

Row 3: P2, twist 2 right, K1 through back loop, twist 2 left, P2.

Row 4: K2, (P1 through back loop, K1) twice, P1 through back loop, K2.

Row 5: P1, twist 2 right, P1, K1 through back loop, P1, twist 2 left, P1.

Row 6: K1, (P1 through back loop, K2) twice, P1 through back loop, K1.

Row 7: Twist 2 right, P1, K next 3 sts through back loop, P1, twist 2 left.

Row 8: P1 through back loop, K2, P next 3 sts through back loop, K2, P1 through back loop.

Rep these 8 rows.

AUGUST
24

Three-Stitch Twisted Rib

Multiple of 5 + 2
Row 1: K2, *P3, K2; rep from * to end.
Row 2 (right side): P2, *cross 3, P2; rep from * to end.
Rep these 2 rows.

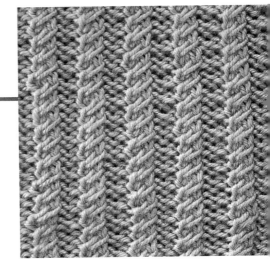

MAY
3

Gate and Ladder Pattern

Multiple of 9 + 3

Row 1: Purl.

Row 2 (right side): K1, K2tog, K3, YO twice, K3, *K3tog, K3, YO twice, K3; rep from * to last 3 sts, K2tog, K1.

Row 3: P6, K1, *P8, K1; rep from * to last 5 sts, P5.

Rep Rows 2 and 3 throughout.

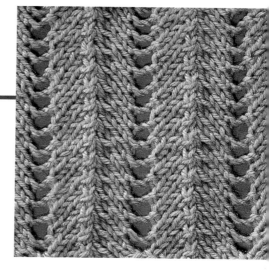

AUGUST
23

Sailors' Rib

Multiple of 5 + 1

Row 1 (right side): K1 through back loop, *P1, K2, P1, K1 through back loop; rep from * to end.

Row 2: P1, *K1, P2, K1, P1; rep from * to end.

Row 3: K1 through back loop, *P4, K1 through back loop; rep from * to end.

Row 4: P1, *K4, P1; rep from * to end.

Rep these 4 rows.

MAY
4

Woven Cables in Relief

Multiple of 15 + 2

Row 1 (right side): Knit.

Row 2: Purl.

Row 3: K1, cable 10 front, *K5, cable 10 front; rep from * to last 6 sts, K6.

Rows 4–8: Work in St st, starting with purl row.

Row 9: K6, cable 10 back, *K5, cable 10 back; rep from * to last st, K1.

Rows 10–12: Work in St st, starting with purl row.

Rep these 12 rows.

Textured Ribbing

Multiple of 6 + 3

Row 1: P3, *K3, P3; rep from * to end.

Row 2 (right side): K3, *P1, wyib, sl 1 knitwise, P1, K3; rep from * to end.

Rows 3–6: Rep Rows 1 and 2 twice more.

Row 7: Knit.

Row 8: P4, *wyib, sl 1 knitwise, P5; rep from * to last 5 sts, wyib, sl 1 knitwise, P4.

Rep these 8 rows.

MAY
5

Allover Lattice Stitch

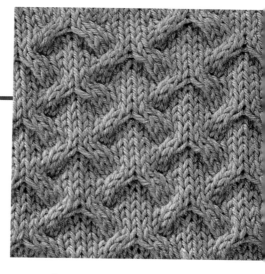

Multiple of 12 + 2

Row 1: Purl.

Row 2 (right side): Knit.

Row 3: Purl.

Row 4: K1, *cable 4 back, K4, cable 4 front; rep from * to last st, K1.

Rows 5–7: Work in St st, starting with purl row.

Row 8: K3, cable 4 front, cable 4 back, *K4, cable 4 front, cable 4 back; rep from * to last 3 sts, K3.

Rep these 8 rows.

August 21

Raised Brick Stitch

Multiple of 4 + 3
Row 1 (right side): K3, *sl 1, K3; rep from * to end.
Row 2: K3, *sl 1 wyif, K3; rep from * to end.
Row 3: K1, sl 1, *K3, sl 1; rep from * to last st, K1.
Row 4: K1, sl 1 wyif, *K3, sl 1 wyif; rep from * to last st, K1.
Rep these 4 rows.

May
6

Woven Lattice Pattern

Multiple of 6 + 2

Row 1: K3, P4, *K2, P4; rep from * to last st, K1.

Row 2 (right side): P1, cable 4 front, *P2, cable 4 front; rep from * to last 3 sts, P3.

Row 3: Rep Row 1.

Row 4: P3, *K2, twist 4 back; rep from * to last 5 sts, K4, P1.

Row 5: K1, P4, *K2, P4; rep from * to last 3 sts, K3.

Row 6: P3, cable 4 back, *P2, cable 4 back; rep from * to last st, P1.

Row 7: Rep Row 5.

Row 8: P1, K4, *twist 4 front, K2; rep from * to last 3 sts, P3.

Rep these 8 rows.

AUGUST
20

Grand Eyelets

Multiple of 4
Row 1: P2, *YO, P4tog; rep from * to last 2 sts, P2.
Row 2: K3, (K1, P1, K1) into next st, *K1, (K1, P1, K1)
into next st; rep from * to last 2 sts, K2.
Row 3: Knit.
Rep these 3 rows.

MAY
7

Four-Stitch Cable 2

Done on a background of reverse St st

Row 1 (right side): Knit.
Row 2: Purl.
Row 3: Cable 4 back.
Row 4: Purl.
Rep these 4 rows.

These instructions result in a cable that twists to the right (shown at right in photo). To twist the cable to the left (shown at left in photo), hold the cable to the front instead of the back in Row 3.

AUGUST
19

Diagonal Openwork

Multiple of 4 + 2

Row 1 (right side): *K1, YO, sl 1, K2tog, psso, YO; rep from * to last 2 sts, K2.

Row 2 and every even row: Purl.

Row 3: K2, *YO, sl 1, K2tog, psso, YO, K1; rep from * to end.

Row 5: K2tog, YO, K1, YO, *sl 1, K2tog, psso, YO, K1, YO; rep from * to last 3 sts, sl 1, K1, psso, K1.

Row 7: K1, K2tog, YO, K1, YO, *sl 1, K2tog, psso, YO, K1, YO; rep from * to last 2 sts, sl 1, K1, psso.

Row 8: Rep Row 2.

Rep these 8 rows.

MAY
8

Six-Stitch Braid

Done on a background of reverse St st

Upward Braid (shown at left in photo)
Row 1 (right side): Cable 4 back, K2.
Row 2: Purl.
Row 3: K2, cable 4 front.
Row 4: Purl.
Rep these 4 rows.

Downward Braid (shown at right in photo)
Row 1 (right side): Cable 4 front, K2.
Row 2: Purl.
Row 3: K2, cable 4 back.
Row 4: Purl.
Rep these 4 rows.

AUGUST
18

Cell Stitch

Multiple of 4 + 3
Row 1 (right side): K2, *YO, sl 1, K2tog, psso, YO, K1; rep from * to last st, K1.
Row 2: Purl.
Row 3: K1, K2tog, YO, K1, *YO, sl 1, K2tog, psso, YO, K1; rep from * to last 3 sts, YO, sl 1, K1, psso, K1.
Row 4: Purl.
Rep these 4 rows.

MAY
9

Nine-Stitch Braid

Done on a background of reverse St st

Upward Braid (shown at left in photo)
Row 1 (right side): Knit.
Row 2 and every even row: Purl.
Row 3: Cable 6 back, K3.
Row 5: Knit.
Row 7: K3, cable 6 front.
Row 8: Purl.
Rep these 8 rows.

Downward Braid (shown at right in photo)
Row 1 (right side): Knit.
Row 2 and every even row: Purl.
Row 3: Cable 6 front, K3.
Row 5: Knit.
Row 7: K3, cable 6 back.
Row 8: Purl.
Rep these 8 rows.

AUGUST
17

Claw Pattern 1

Worked over 8 sts on a background of reverse St st

Upward Claw (shown at left in photo)
Row 1 (right side): Knit.
Row 2: Purl.
Row 3: Cable 4 back, cable 4 front.
Row 4: Purl.
Rep these 4 rows.

Downward Claw (shown at right in photo)
Row 1 (right side): Knit.
Row 2: Purl.
Row 3: Cable 4 front, cable 4 back.
Row 4: Purl.
Rep these 4 rows.

MAY
10

Seeded Rib

Multiple of 4 + 1
Row 1 (right side): P1, *K3, P1; rep from * to end.
Row 2: K2, P1, *K3, P1; rep from * to last 2 sts, K2.
Rep these 2 rows.

AUGUST
16

Claw Pattern 2

Worked over 9 sts on a background of reverse St st

Upward Claw (shown at left in photo)
Row 1 (right side): Knit.
Row 2: Purl.
Row 3: Cross 4 right, K1, cross 4 left.
Row 4: Purl.
Rep these 4 rows.

Downward Claw (shown at right in photo)
Row 1 (right side): Knit.
Row 2: Purl.
Row 3: Cross 4 left, K1, cross 4 right.
Row 4: Purl.
Rep these 4 rows.

MAY
11

Blanket Rib

Multiple of 2 + 1

Row 1 (right side): Knit into front and back of each st (thus doubling the number of sts).

Row 2: K2tog, *P2tog, K2tog; rep from * to end (original number of sts restored).

Rep these 2 rows.

AUGUST
15

Double Cable

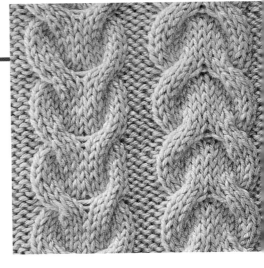

Worked over 12 sts on a background of reverse St st

Upward Cable (shown at left in photo)
Row 1 (right side): Knit.
Row 2: Purl.
Row 3: Cable 6 back, cable 6 front.
Row 4: Purl.
Rows 5–8: Rep Rows 1 and 2 twice more.
Rep these 8 rows.

Downward Cable (shown at right in photo)
Row 1 (right side): Knit.
Row 2: Purl.
Row 3: Cable 6 front, cable 6 back.
Row 4: Purl.
Rows 5–8: Rep Rows 1 and 2 twice more.
Rep these 8 rows.

MAY
12

Shadow Rib

Multiple of 3 + 2
Row 1 (right side): Knit.
Row 2: P2, *K1 through back loop, P2; rep from * to end.
Rep these 2 rows.

AUGUST
14

Branched Cable 1

Worked over 10 sts on a background of reverse St st

Row 1 (right side): P3, cable 4 back, P3.

Row 2: K3, P4, K3.

Row 3: P2, twist 3 back, twist 3 front, P2.

Row 4: (K2, P2) twice, K2.

Row 5: P1, twist 3 back, P2, twist 3 front, P1.

Row 6: K1, P2, K4, P2, K1.

Row 7: Twist 3 back, P4, twist 3 front.

Row 8: P2, K6, P2.

Rep these 8 rows.

MAY
13

Random Dash Pattern

Odd-number multiple of 6 + 1**

Row 1 (right side): K1, *P2, K1; rep from * to end.
Row 2: P1, *K2, P1; rep from * to end.
Rows 3 and 4: Rep Rows 1 and 2.
Row 5: K1, *P5, K1; rep from * to end.
Row 6: P1, *K5, P1; rep from * to end.
Rows 7 and 8: Rep Rows 5 and 6.
Row 9 and 11: Rep Row 1.
Row 10 and 12: Rep Row 2.
Row 13: P3, *K1, P3; rep from * to end.
Row 14: K3, *P1, K3; rep from * to end.
Rows 15 and 16: Rep Rows 13 and 14.
Rep these 16 rows.

**For example, 6x3, 6x5, 6x7, etc.

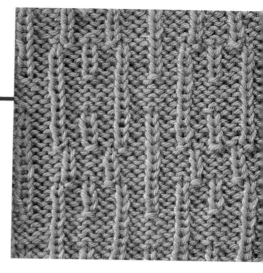

AUGUST
13

Diagonals

Multiple of 8 + 6

Row 1 (right side): P3, *K5, P3; rep from * to last 3 sts, K3.

Row 2: P4, *K3, P5, rep from * to last 2 sts, K2.

Row 3: P1, K5, *P3, K5; rep from * to end.

Row 4: K1, P5, *K3, P5; rep from * to end.

Row 5: K4, *P3, K5; rep from * to last 2 sts, P2.

Row 6: K3, *P5, K3; rep from * to last 3 sts, P3.

Row 7: K2, P3, *K5, P3; rep from * to last st, K1.

Row 8: P2, K3, *P5, K3; rep from * to last st, P1.

Rep these 8 rows.

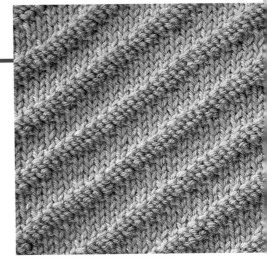

MAY
14

Vertical Dash Stitch

Multiple of 6 + 1

Row 1 (right side): P3, K1, *P5, K1; rep from * to last 3 sts, P3.

Row 2: K3, P1, *K5, P1; rep from * to last 3 sts, K3.

Rows 3 and 4: Rep Rows 1 and 2.

Row 5: K1, *P5, K1; rep from * to end.

Row 6: P1, *K5, P1; rep from * to end.

Rows 7 and 8: Rep Rows 5 and 6.

Rep these 8 rows.

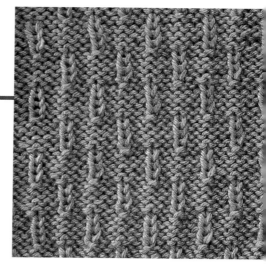

AUGUST
12

Caterpillar Stitch

Multiple of 8 + 6
Row 1 (right side): K4, P2, *K6, P2; rep from * to end.
Row 2: P1, K2, *P6, K2; rep from * to last 3 sts, P3.
Row 3: K2, P2, *K6, P2; rep from * to last 2 sts, K2.
Row 4: P3, K2, *P6, K2; rep from * to last st, P1.
Row 5: P2, *K6, P2; rep from * to last 4 sts, K4.
Row 6: Purl.
Rep these 6 rows.

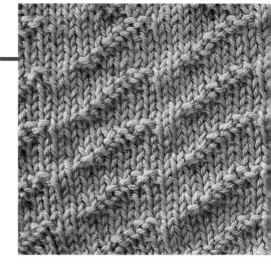

MAY
15

Oblong Texture

Multiple of 10 + 1

Row 1 (right side): K3, P5, *K5, P5; rep from * to last 3 sts, K3.

Row 2: P3, K5, *P5, K5; rep from * to last 3 sts, P3.

Row 3: Rep Row 2.

Row 4: Rep Row 1.

Rep these 4 rows.

AUGUST
11

Diamond Pattern

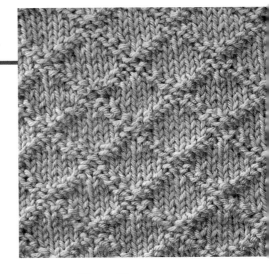

Multiple of 8 + 1

Row 1 (right side): P1, *K7, P1; rep from * to end.

Row 2: K2, P5, *K3, P5; rep from * to last 2 sts, K2.

Row 3: K1, *P2, K3, P2, K1; rep from * to end.

Row 4: P2, K2, P1, K2, *P3, K2, P1, K2; rep from * to last 2 sts, P2.

Row 5: K3, P3, *K5, P3; rep from * to last 3 sts, K3.

Row 6: P4, K1, *P7, K1; rep from * to last 4 sts, P4.

Row 7: Rep Row 5.

Row 8: Rep Row 4.

Row 9: Rep Row 3.

Row 10: Rep Row 2.

Rep these 10 rows.

MAY
16

Knotted Cable

Worked over 6 sts on a background of reverse St st

Row 1 (right side): K2, P2, K2.

Row 2 and every even row: P2, K2, P2.

Row 3: Cross 6.

Rows 5, 7, and 9: Rep Row 1.

Row 10: Rep Row 2.

Rep these 10 rows.

AUGUST
10

Medallion Cable

Worked over 13 sts on a background of reverse St st

Row 1 (right side): Knit.
Row 2: Purl.
Rows 3 and 4: Rep Rows 1 and 2.
Row 5: Cable 6 front, K1, cable 6 back.
Row 6: Rep Row 2.
Row 7: Rep Row 1.
Rows 8–11: Rep Rows 6 and 7 twice more.
Row 12: Rep Row 2.
Row 13: Cable 6 back, K1, cable 6 front.
Row 14: Rep Row 2.
Row 15: Rep Row 1.
Row 16: Rep Row 2.
Rep these 16 rows.

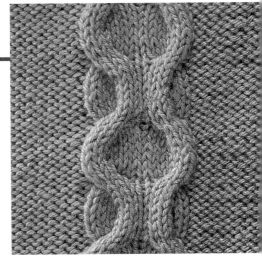

MAY
17

Cable Circles

Worked over 12 sts on a background of reverse St st

Row 1 (right side): Purl.

Row 2: Knit.

Row 3: P3, K6, P3.

Row 4: K3, P6, K3.

Row 5: Cable 6 back, cable 6 front.

Rows 6–10: Work in St st, starting with purl row.

Row 11: Twist 6 front, twist 6 back.

Row 12: Rep Row 4.

Rep these 12 rows.

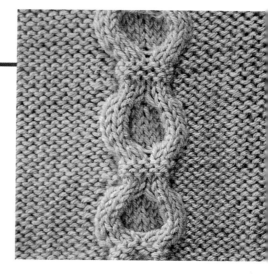

AUGUST
9

Staghorn Cable 1

Worked over 16 sts on a background of reverse St st
Row 1 (right side): K4, cable 4 back, cable 4 front, K4.
Row 2: Purl.
Row 3: K2, cable 4 back, K4, cable 4 front, K2.
Row 4: Purl.
Row 5: Cable 4 back, K8, cable 4 front.
Row 6: Purl.
Rep these 6 rows.

MAY
18

Garter and Stockinette Cable

Worked over 8 sts on a background of reverse St st
Row 1 (right side): Knit.
Row 2: P4, K4.
Rows 3–6: Rep Rows 1 and 2 twice.
Row 7: Cable 8 back.
Row 8: K4, P4.
Row 9: Knit.
Rows 10–18: Rep Rows 8 and 9 four more times; then rep Row 8 again.
Row 19: Cable 8 back.
Row 20: Rep Row 2.
Row 21: Knit.
Rows 22–24: Rep Rows 20 and 21; then rep Row 20 again.
Rep these 24 rows.

AUGUST
8

Staghorn Cable 2

Worked over 16 sts on a background of reverse St st
Row 1 (right side): Cable 4 front, K8, cable 4 back.
Row 2: Purl.
Row 3: K2, cable 4 front, K4, cable 4 back, K2.
Row 4: Purl.
Row 5: K4, cable 4 front, cable 4 back, K4.
Row 6: Purl.
Rep these 6 rows.

MAY
19

Honeycomb Pattern

Worked over a multiple of 8 sts on a background of reverse St st. The example shown is worked over 24 sts.

Row 1 (right side): *Cable 4 back, cable 4 front; rep from * to end of panel.

Row 2 and every even row: Purl.

Row 3: Knit.

Row 5: *Cable 4 front, cable 4 back; rep from * to end of panel.

Row 7: Knit.

Row 8: Purl.

Rep these 8 rows.

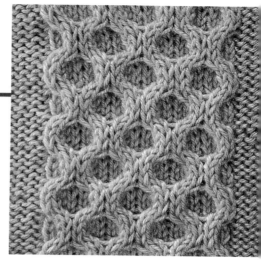

AUGUST
7

Little Arrows

Multiple of 8 + 1
Row 1 (right side): K2, P2, K1, P2, *K3, P2, K1, P2; rep from * to last 2 sts, K2.
Row 2: P3, K1, P1, K1, *P5, K1, P1, K1; rep from * to last 3 sts, P3.
Row 3: K1, *P1, K5, P1, K1; rep from * to end.
Row 4: P1, *K2, P3, K2, P1; rep from * to end.
Rep these 4 rows.

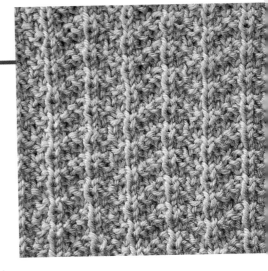

MAY
20

Honeycomb Cable

Worked over 12 sts on a background of reverse St st

Row 1 (right side): K4, cross 2 front, cross 2 back, K4.
Row 2 and every even row: Purl.
Row 3: K2, (cross 2 front, cross 2 back) twice, K2.
Row 5: (Cross 2 front, cross 2 back) 3 times.
Row 7: (Cross 2 back, cross 2 front) 3 times.
Row 9: K2, (cross 2 back, cross 2 front) twice, K2.
Row 11: K4, cross 2 back, cross 2 front, K4.
Row 12: Rep Row 2.
Rep these 12 rows.

AUGUST
6

Little Arrowhead

Multiple of 6 + 1

Row 1 (right side): K1, *YO, sl 1, K1, psso, K1, K2tog, YO, K1; rep from * to end.

Row 2: Purl.

Row 3: K2, *YO, sl 1, K2tog, psso, YO, K3; rep from * to last 5 sts, YO, sl 1, K2tog, psso, YO, K2.

Row 4: Purl.

Rep these 4 rows.

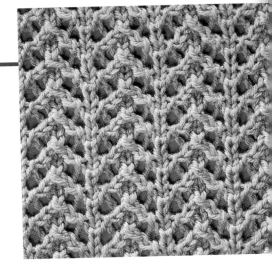

MAY
21

Diamond Rib

Multiple of 9 + 2

Row 1 (right side): P2, *K2tog, (K1, YO) twice, K1, sl 1, K1, psso, P2; rep from * to end.

Row 2 and every even row: K2, *P7, K2; rep from * to end.

Row 3: P2, *K2tog, YO, K3, YO, sl 1, K1, psso, P2; rep from * to end.

Row 5: P2, *K1, YO, sl 1, K1, psso, K1, K2tog, YO, K1, P2; rep from * to end.

Row 7: P2, *K2, YO, sl 1, K2tog, psso, YO, K2, P2; rep from * to end.

Row 8: Rep Row 2.

Rep these 8 rows.

AUGUST
5

Banded Rib

Multiple of 2 + 1
Row 1 (right side): K1, *P1, K1; rep from * to end.
Row 2: P1, *K1, P1; rep from * to end.
Rows 3–6: Rep Rows 1 and 2 twice more.
Row 7: P1, *K1, P1; rep from * to end.
Row 8: K1, *P1, K1; rep from * to end.
Rows 9–12: Rep Rows 7 and 8 twice more.
Rep these 12 rows.

MAY
22

Bell Lace

Multiple of 8 + 3

Row 1 (right side): K1, P1, K1, *P1, YO, sl 1, K2tog, psso, YO, (P1, K1) twice; rep from * to end.

Row 2: P1, K1, P1, *K1, P3, (K1, P1) twice; rep from * to end.

Rows 3–6: Rep Rows 1 and 2 twice.

Row 7: K1, K2tog, *YO, (P1, K1) twice, P1, YO, sl 1, K2tog, psso; rep from * to last 8 sts, YO, (P1, K1) twice, P1, YO, sl 1, K1, psso, K1.

Row 8: P3, *(K1, P1) twice, K1, P3; rep from * to end.

Rows 9–12: Rep Rows 7 and 8 twice.

Rep these 12 rows.

AUGUST
4

Ridged Openwork

Multiple of 2 + 1

Row 1 (right side): Purl.

Row 2: *P2tog; rep from * to last st, P1.

Row 3: P1, *purl through horizontal strand of yarn lying between stitch just worked and next st, P1; rep from * to end.

Row 4: P1, *YO, P2tog; rep from * to end.

Rep these 4 rows.

May
23

Fancy Openwork

Multiple of 4

Row 1 (right side): K2, *YO, K4; rep from * to last 2 sts, YO, K2.

Row 2: P2tog, *(K1, P1) into YO from previous row, P2tog twice; rep from * to last 3 sts, (K1, P1) into YO from previous row, P2tog.

Row 3: K4, *YO, K4; rep from * to end.

Row 4: P2, P2tog, *(K1, P1) into YO from previous row, P2tog twice; rep from * to last 5 sts, (K1, P1) into YO from previous row, P2tog, P2.

Rep these 4 rows.

AUGUST
3

Ridged Eyelet Border

Multiple of 2 + 1
Worked on a background of St st
Rows 1–3: Knit.
Row 4 (wrong side): *P2tog, YO; rep from * to last st, P1.
Rows 5–7: Knit.
Row 8: Purl.
Rows 9–16: Rep Rows 1–8.
Row 17: Knit.
Row 18: Purl.
Row 19: Knit.
Row 20: Purl.
Rep these 20 rows.

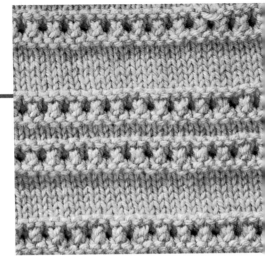

MAY
24

Faggoting

Multiple of 3

Row 1 (right side): *K1, YO twice, K2tog; rep from * to end.

Row 2: P1, *purl into first YO of previous row, drop 2nd YO off needle, P2; rep from * to last 3 sts, purl into first YO, drop 2nd YO off needle, P1.

Row 3: *K2tog, YO twice, K1; rep from * to end.

Row 4: Rep Row 2.

Rep these 4 rows.

AUGUST
2

Twist Motif

Multiple of 16 + 2

Rows 1–4: Work in St st, starting with knit row.

Row 5 (right side): K7, cross 2 front, cross 2 back, *K12, cross 2 front, cross 2 back; rep from * to last 7 sts, K7.

Row 6: Purl.

Row 7: K7, cross 2 back, cross 2 front, *K12, cross 2 back, cross 2 front; rep from * to last 7 sts, K7.

Rows 8–14: Work in St st, starting with purl row.

Row 15: K1, *cross 2 back, K12, cross 2 front; rep from * to last st, K1.

Row 16: Purl.

Row 17: K1, *cross 2 front, K12, cross 2 back; rep from * to last st, K1.

Rows 18–20: Work in St st, starting with purl row.

Rep these 20 rows.

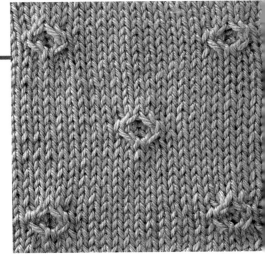

MAY
25

Lace Check

Multiple of 18 + 9

Row 1: Purl.

Row 2 (right side): K1, *(YO, K2tog) 4 times, K10; rep from * to last 8 sts, (YO, K2tog) 4 times.

Row 3: Purl.

Row 4: *(Sl 1, K1, psso, YO) 4 times, K10; rep from * to last 9 sts, (sl 1, K1, psso, YO) 4 times, K1.

Rows 5–12: Rep Rows 1–4 twice.

Row 13: Purl.

Row 14: *K10, (YO, K2tog) 4 times; rep from * to last 9 sts, K9.

Row 15: Purl.

Row 16: K9, *(sl 1, K1, psso, YO) 4 times, K10; rep from * to end.

Rows 17–24: Rep Rows 13–16 twice.

Rep these 24 rows.

AUGUST
1

Cable and Box Panel

Worked over 8 sts on a background of reverse St st

Row 1 (right side): Knit.

Row 2: Purl.

Row 3: Cable 8 front.

Rows 4–7: Work in St st, starting with purl row.

Row 8: P2, K4, P2.

Row 9: K2, P4, K2.

Rows 10–13: Rep Rows 8 and 9 twice more.

Rows 14–16: Work in St st, starting with purl row.

Rep these 16 rows.

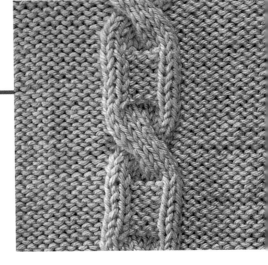

MAY
26

Alternating Lace

Multiple of 6 + 5

Row 1 (right side): K1, *YO, sl 1, K2tog, psso, YO, K3; rep from * to last 4 sts, YO, sl 1, K2tog, psso, YO, K1.

Row 2: Purl.

Rows 3–8: Rep Rows 1 and 2 three more times.

Row 9: K4, *YO, sl 1, K2tog, psso, YO, K3; rep from * to last st, K1.

Row 10: Purl.

Rows 11–16: Rep Rows 9 and 10 three more times.

Rep these 16 rows.

JULY
31

Squares and Twists

Multiple of 10 + 4

Row 1: P4, *K2, P2, K2, P4; rep from * to end.

Row 2 (right side): K4, *P2, cross 2 front, P2, K4; rep from * to end.

Rows 3 and 4: Rep Rows 1 and 2.

Row 5: K1, P2, *K2, P4, K2, P2; rep from * to last st, K1.

Row 6: P1, cross 2 front, *P2, K4, P2, cross 2 front; rep from * to last st, P1.

Rows 7 and 8: Rep Rows 5 and 6.

Rep these 8 rows.

MAY
27

Twist Cable and Ladder Lace

Multiple of 7 + 6

Row 1 (right side): K1, *K2tog, YO twice, sl 1, K1, psso, K3; rep from * to last 5 sts, K2tog, YO twice, sl 1, K1, psso, K1.

Row 2: K2, *(K1, K1 through back loop) into double YO of previous row, K1, P3, K1; rep from * to last 4 sts, (K1, K1 through back loop) into double YO of previous row, K2.

Row 3: K1, *K2tog, YO twice, sl 1, K1, psso, knit into 3rd st on left-hand needle, then knit into 2nd st, then knit into first st, slipping all 3 sts onto right-hand needle tog; rep from * to last 5 sts, K2tog, YO twice, sl 1, K1, psso, K1.

Row 4: Rep Row 2.

Rep these 4 rows.

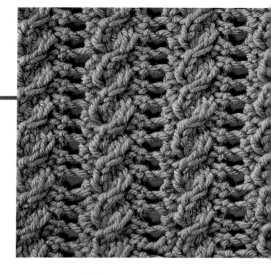

JULY
30

Slip-Stitch Stripes

Multiple of 5

Row 1 (wrong side): K2, *P1, K4; rep from * to last 3 sts, P1, K2.

Row 2: K2, *sl 1, K4; rep from * to last 3 sts, sl 1, K2.

Rep these 2 rows.

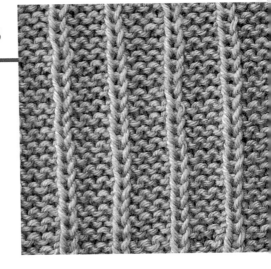

MAY
28

Lacy Diamonds

Multiple of 6 + 1

Row 1 (right side): *K1, K2tog, YO, K1, YO, K2tog through back loop; rep from * to last st, K1.

Row 2 and every even row: Purl.

Row 3: K2tog, *YO, K3, YO, sl 1 twice, K1, p2sso; rep from * to last 5 sts, YO, K3, YO, K2tog through back loop.

Row 5: *K1, YO, K2tog through back loop, K1, K2tog, YO; rep from * to last st, K1.

Row 7: K2, *YO, sl 1 twice, K1, p2sso, YO, K3; rep from * to last 5 sts, YO, sl 1 twice, K1, p2sso, YO, K2.

Row 8: Rep Row 2.

Rep these 8 rows.

JULY
29

Slip-Stitch Ribbing

Multiple of 8 + 3

Row 1 (right side): P3, *K1 (wrapping yarn twice around needle), P3, K1, P3; rep from * to end.

Row 2: K3, *P1, K3, sl 1 wyif (dropping extra loop), K3; rep from * to end.

Row 3: P3, *sl 1 wyib, P3, K1, P3; rep from * to end.

Row 4: K3, *P1, K3, sl 1 wyif, K3; rep from * to end.

Rep these 4 rows.

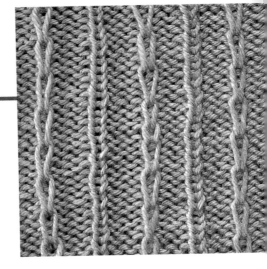

MAY
29

Fern Lace

Multiple of 9 + 4

Row 1: Purl.

Row 2 (right side): K3, *YO, K2, sl 1, K1, psso, K2tog, K2, YO, K1; rep from * to last st, K1.

Row 3: Purl.

Row 4: K2, *YO, K2, sl 1, K1, psso, K2tog, K2, YO, K1; rep from * to last 2 sts, K2.

Rep these 4 rows.

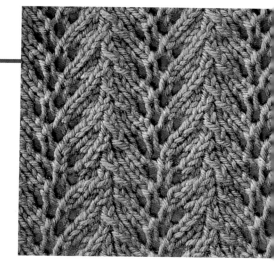

JULY
28

Zigzag Eyelet Panel

Worked over 11 sts on a background of St st
Row 1 (right side): K6, YO, sl 1, K1, psso, K3.
Row 2 and every even row: Purl.
Row 3: K7, YO, sl 1, K1, psso, K2.
Row 5: K3, K2tog, YO, K3, YO, sl 1, K1, psso, K1.
Row 7: K2, K2tog, YO, K5, YO, sl 1, K1, psso.
Row 9: K1, K2tog, YO, K8.
Row 11: K2tog, YO, K9.
Row 12: Rep Row 2.
Rep these 12 rows.

MAY
30

Houndstooth Tweed

Multiple of 3
Cast on in color A.
Row 1 (right side): Using color A, *K2, sl 1; rep from * to end.
Row 2: Using color A, knit.
Row 3: Using color B, *sl 1, K2; rep from * to end.
Row 4: Using color B, knit.
Rep these 4 rows.

JULY
27

Fish-Scale Lace Panel

Worked over 17 sts on a background of St st

Row 1 (right side): K1, YO, K3, sl 1, K1, psso, P5, K2tog, K3, YO, K1.
Row 2: P6, K5, P6.
Row 3: K2, YO, K3, sl 1, K1, psso, P3, K2tog, K3, YO, K2.
Row 4: P7, K3, P7.
Row 5: K3, YO, K3, sl 1, K1, psso, P1, K2tog, K3, YO, K3.
Row 6: P8, K1, P8.
Row 7: K4, YO, K3, sl 1, K2tog, psso, K3, YO, K4.
Row 8: Purl.
Rep these 8 rows.

MAY
31

Twisted Knit Tweed

Multiple of 2 + 1
Using color A, knit 2 foundation rows.
Row 1 (right side): Using color B, K1, *K1 in st below, K1; rep from * to end.
Row 2: Using color B, knit.
Row 3: Using color A, K1 in row below, *K1, K1 in st below; rep from * to end.
Row 4: Using color A, knit.
Rep these 4 rows.

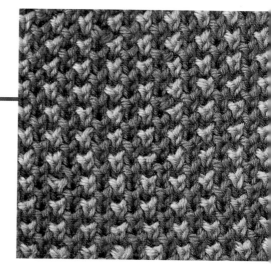

JULY
26

Double Basket Weave

Multiple of 4 + 3
Row 1 and every odd row (right side): Knit.
Row 2: *K3, P1; rep from * to last 3 sts, K3.
Row 4: Rep Row 2.
Row 6: K1, *P1, K3; rep from * to last 2 sts, P1, K1.
Row 8: Rep Row 6.
Rep these 8 rows.

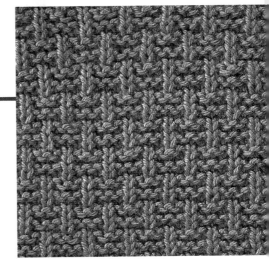

JUNE
1

Double Rice Stitch

Multiple of 2 + 1

Row 1: P1, *K1 through back loop, P1; rep from * to end.

Row 2 (right side): Knit.

Row 3: *K1 through back loop, P1; rep from * to last st, K1 through back loop.

Row 4: Knit.

Rep these 4 rows.

JULY
25

Woven Stitch 1

Multiple of 4 + 2
Row 1 (right side): Knit.
Row 2: Purl.
Row 3: K2, *P2, K2; rep from * to end.
Row 4: P2, *K2, P2; rep from * to end.
Row 5: Knit.
Row 6: Purl.
Row 7: Rep Row 4.
Row 8: Rep Row 3.
Rep these 8 rows.

JUNE
2

Mock Cable: Left

Multiple of 4 + 2
Row 1 (right side): P2, *K2, P2; rep from * to end.
Row 2: K2, *P2, K2; rep from * to end.
Row 3: P2, *cross 2 back, P2; rep from * to end.
Row 4: Rep Row 2.
Rep these 4 rows.

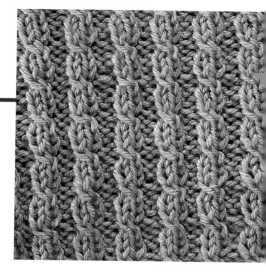

JULY
24

Check Stitch

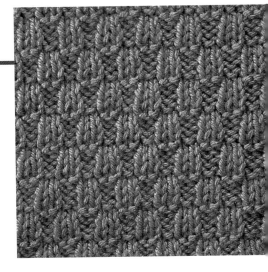

Multiple of 4 + 2
Row 1 (right side): K2, *P2, K2; rep from * to end.
Row 2: P2, *K2, P2; rep from * to end.
Row 3: Rep Row 1.
Row 4: Rep Row 2.
Row 5: Rep Row 2.
Row 6: Rep Row 1.
Row 7: Rep Row 2.
Row 8: Rep Row 1.
Rep these 8 rows.

JUNE
3

Mock Cable: Right

Multiple of 4 + 2
Row 1 (right side): P2, *K2, P2; rep from * to end.
Row 2: K2, *P2, K2; rep from * to end.
Row 3: P2, *cross 2 front, P2; rep from * to end.
Row 4: Rep Row 2.
Rep these 4 rows.

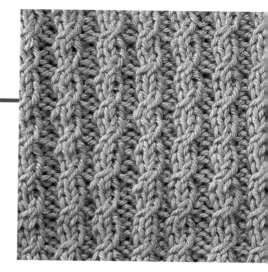

Mosaic Stitch

Multiple of 10 + 7

Row 1 (right side): P3, *K1, P3, K1, P1, K1, P3; rep from * to last 4 sts, K1, P3.

Row 2: K3, *P1, K3, P1, K1, P1, K3; rep from * to last 4 sts, P1, K3.

Row 3: Rep Row 1.

Row 4: Rep Row 2.

Row 5: P2, *K1, P1, K1, P3, K1, P3; rep from * to last 5 sts, K1, P1, K1, P2.

Row 6: K2, *P1, K1, P1, K3, P1, K3; rep from * to last 5 sts, P1, K1, P1, K2.

Row 7: Rep Row 5.

Row 8: Rep Row 6.

Rep these 8 rows.

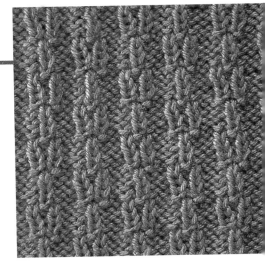

JUNE
4

Garter-Stitch Eyelet Chevron

Multiple of 9 + 1

Row 1 (right side): K1, *YO, sl 1, K1, psso, K4, K2tog, YO, K1; rep from * to end.

Row 2: P2, *K6, P3; rep from * to last 8 sts, K6, P2.

Row 3: K2, *YO, sl 1, K1, psso, K2, K2tog, YO, K3; rep from * to last 8 sts, YO, sl 1, K1, psso, K2, K2tog, YO, K2.

Row 4: P3, *K4, P5; rep from * to last 7 sts, K4, P3.

Row 5: K3, *YO, sl 1, K1, psso, K2tog, YO, K5; rep from * to last 7 sts, YO, sl 1, K1, psso, K2tog, YO, K3.

Row 6: P4, *K2, P7; rep from * to last 6 sts, K2, P4.

Rep these 6 rows.

JULY
22

Ladder Stitch

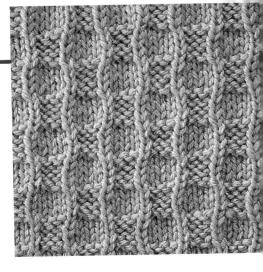

Multiple of 8 + 5

Row 1 (right side): K5, *P3, K5; rep from * to end.

Row 2: P5, *K3, P5; rep from * to end.

Row 3: Rep Row 1.

Row 4: Rep Row 2.

Row 5: K1, *P3, K5; rep from * to last 4 sts, P3, K1.

Row 6: P1, *K3, P5; rep from * to last 4 sts, K3, P1.

Row 7: Rep Row 5.

Row 8: Rep Row 6.

Rep these 8 rows.

JUNE
5

Hourglass Eyelets

Multiple of 6 + 1

Row 1 (right side): K6, *P1, K5; rep from * to last st, K1.

Row 2: K1, *P5, K1; rep from * to end.

Row 3: K1, *YO, sl 1, K1, psso, P1, K2tog, YO, K1; rep from * to end.

Row 4: K1, P2, *K1, P5; rep from * to last 4 sts, K1, P2, K1.

Row 5: K3, *P1, K5; rep from * to last 4 sts, P1, K3.

Row 6: Rep Row 4.

Row 7: K1, *K2tog, YO, K1, YO, sl 1, K1, psso, P1; rep from * to last 6 sts, K2tog, YO, K1, YO, sl 1, K1, psso, K1.

Row 8: Rep Row 2.

Rep these 8 rows.

JULY
21

Pennant Stitch

Multiple of 5
Row 1 (right side): Knit.
Row 2: *K1, P4; rep from * to end.
Row 3: *K3, P2; rep from * to end.
Row 4: Rep Row 3.
Row 5: Rep Row 2.
Rows 6 and 7: Knit.
Row 8: *P4, K1; rep from * to end.
Row 9: *P2, K3; rep from * to end.
Row 10: Rep Row 9.
Row 11: Rep Row 8.
Row 12: Knit.
Rep these 12 rows.

JUNE
6

Small Cable Check

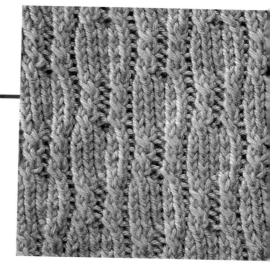

Multiple of 12 + 7

Row 1 (right side): *P1, K next 5 sts through back loop, (P1, cross 2 front) twice; rep from * to last 7 sts, P1, K next 5 sts through back loop, P1.

Row 2: *K1, P next 5 sts through back loop, (K1, P2) twice; rep from * to last 7 sts, K1, P next 5 sts through back loop, K1.

Rows 3–6: Rep Rows 1 and 2 twice.

Row 7: *(P1, cross 2 front) twice, P1, K next 5 sts through back loop; rep from * to last 7 sts, (P1, cross 2 front) twice, P1.

Row 8: *(K1, P2) twice, K1, P next 5 sts through back loop; rep from * to last 7 sts, (K1, P2) twice, K1.

Rows 9–12: Rep Rows 7 and 8 twice.

Rep these 12 rows.

JULY
20

Check Pattern

Multiple of 3 + 1
Row 1 (right side): Knit.
Row 2: Purl.
Row 3: K1, *P2, K1; rep from * to end.
Row 4: Purl.
Rep these 4 rows.

JUNE
7

Double Mock Rib

Multiple of 4 + 2
Row 1 (right side): K2, *P2, K2; rep from * to end.
Row 2: P2, *sl 2 wyif, P2; rep from * to end.
Rep these 2 rows.

JULY
19

Close Checks

Multiple of 6 + 3
Row 1 (right side): K3, *P3, K3; rep from * to end.
Row 2: P3, *K3, P3; rep from * to end.
Row 3: Rep Row 1.
Row 4: Rep Row 2.
Row 5: Rep Row 2.
Row 6: Rep Row 1.
Row 7: Rep Row 2.
Row 8: Rep Row 1.
Rep these 8 rows.

June
8

Mock Rib

Multiple of 2 + 1
Row 1 (right side): K1, *P1, K1; rep from * to end.
Row 2: P1, *sl 1 wyif, P1; rep from * to end.
Rep these 2 rows.

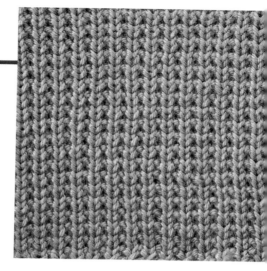

JULY
18

Spaced Checks

Multiple of 10 + 1
Row 1: Purl.
Row 2 (right side): K4, *P3, K7; rep from * to last 7 sts, P3, K4.
Row 3: P4, *K3, P7; rep from * to last 7 sts, K3, P4.
Row 4: Rep Row 2.
Row 5: Purl.
Row 6: Knit.
Row 7: K2, *P7, K3; rep from * to last 9 sts, P7, K2.
Row 8: P2, *K7, P3; rep from * to last 9 sts, K7, P2.
Row 9: Rep Row 7.
Row 10: Knit.
Rep these 10 rows.

JUNE
9

Garter-Stitch Checks

Multiple of 10 + 5

Row 1 (right side): K5, *P5, K5; rep from * to end.
Row 2: Purl.
Row 3: Rep Row 1.
Row 4: Rep Row 2.
Row 5: Rep Row 1.
Row 6: Rep Row 1.
Row 7: Knit.
Row 8: Rep Row 1.
Row 9: Rep Row 7.
Row 10: Rep Row 1.
Rep these 10 rows.

July
17

Rib Checks

Multiple of 10 + 5

Row 1 (right side): P5, *(K1 through back loop, P1) twice, K1 through back loop, P5; rep from * to end.

Row 2: K5, *(P1 through back loop, K1) twice, P1 through back loop, K5; rep from * to end.

Row 3: Rep Row 1.

Row 4: Rep Row 2.

Row 5: Rep Row 1.

Row 6: (P1 through back loop, K1) twice, P1 through back loop, *K5, (P1 through back loop, K1) twice, P1 through back loop; rep from * to end.

Row 7: (K1 through back loop, P1) twice, K1 through back loop, *P5, (K1 through back loop, P1) twice, K1 through back loop; rep from * to end.

Row 8: Rep Row 6.

Row 9: Rep Row 7.

Row 10: Rep Row 6.

Rep these 10 rows.

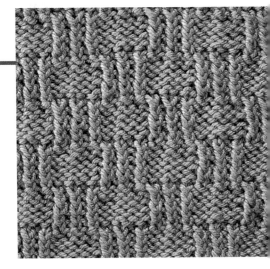

JUNE
10

Bobble Rib

Multiple of 8 + 3

Row 1 (right side): K3, *P2, (P1, K1) twice into next st, pass the first 3 of these sts, one at a time, over the 4th st (bobble made), P2, K3; rep from * to end.

Row 2: P3, *K2, P1, K2, P3; rep from * to end.

Row 3: K3, *P2, K1, P2, K3; rep from * to end.

Row 4: Rep Row 2.

Rep these 4 rows.

JULY
16

Eyelet Mock-Cable Rib

Multiple of 5 + 2
Row 1 (right side): P2, *sl 1, K2, psso, P2; rep from *
to end.
Row 2: K2, *P1, YO, P1, K2; rep from * to end.
Row 3: P2, *K3, P2; rep from * to end.
Row 4: K2, *P3, K2; rep from * to end.
Rep these 4 rows.

JUNE
11

Piqué Rib

Multiple of 10 + 3

Row 1 (right side): K3, *P3, K1, P3, K3; rep from * to end.

Row 2: P3, *K3, P1, K3, P3; rep from * to end.

Row 3: Rep Row 1.

Row 4: Knit.

Rep these 4 rows.

JULY
15

Twisted-Cable Rib

Multiple of 4 + 2

Row 1 (right side): P2, *K2, P2; rep from * to end.

Row 2: K2, *P2, K2; rep from * to end.

Row 3: P2, *K2tog but do not slip off needle, then insert right-hand needle between these 2 sts and knit the first st again, slipping both sts off needle tog, P2; rep from * to end.

Row 4: Rep Row 2.

Rep these 4 rows.

JUNE
12

Open Twisted Rib

Multiple of 5 + 3

Row 1: K1, P1 through back loop, K1, *P2, K1, P1 through back loop, K1; rep from * to end.

Row 2 (right side): P1, K1 through back loop, P1, *K1, YO, K1, P1, K1 through back loop, P1; rep from * to end.

Row 3: K1, P1 through back loop, K1, *P3, K1, P1 through back loop, K1; rep from * to end.

Row 4: P1, K1 through back loop, P1, *K3, pass 3rd st on right-hand needle over first 2 sts, P1, K1 through back loop, P1; rep from * to end.

Rep these 4 rows.

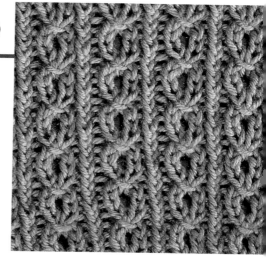

JULY
14

Single-Eyelet Rib

Multiple of 5 + 2
Row 1 (right side): P2, *K3, P2; rep from * to end.
Row 2: K2, *P3, K2; rep from * to end.
Row 3: P2, *K2tog, YO, K1, P2; rep from * to end.
Row 4: Rep Row 2.
Row 5: Rep Row 1.
Row 6: Rep Row 2.
Row 7: P2, *K1, YO, sl 1, K1, psso, P2; rep from * to
end.
Row 8: Rep Row 2.
Rep these 8 rows.

JUNE
13

Single Lace Rib

Multiple of 4 + 1
Row 1 (right side): K1, *YO, K2tog, P1, K1; rep from * to end.
Row 2: P1, *YO, P2tog, K1, P1; rep from * to end.
Rep these 2 rows.

JULY
13

Double-Eyelet Rib

Multiple of 7 + 2
Row 1 (right side): P2, *K5, P2; rep from * to end.
Row 2: K2, *P5, K2; rep from * to end.
Row 3: P2, *K2tog, YO, K1, YO, sl 1, K1, psso, P2; rep from * to end.
Row 4: Rep Row 2.
Rep these 4 rows.

JUNE
14

Knotted Rib

Multiple of 5

Row 1 (right side): P2, *knit into front and back of next st, P4; rep from * to last 3 sts, knit into front and back of next st, P2.

Row 2: K2, *P2tog, K4; rep from * to last 4 sts, P2tog, K2.

Rep these 2 rows.

JULY
12

Piqué Triangles

Multiple of 5
Row 1 (right side): *P1, K4; rep from * to end.
Row 2: *P3, K2; rep from * to end.
Row 3: Rep Row 2.
Row 4: Rep Row 1.
Rep these 4 rows.

JUNE
15

Slipped Rib 2

Multiple of 4 + 3
Row 1 (right side): K1, sl 1, *K3, sl 1; rep from * to last st, K1.
Row 2: P1, sl 1, *P3, sl 1; rep from * to last st, P1.
Row 3: *K3, sl 1; rep from * to last 3 sts, K3.
Row 4: *P3, sl 1; rep from * to last 3 sts, P3.
Rep these 4 rows.

JULY
11

Dash Stitch

Multiple of 6 + 1

Row 1: K3, * P1 through back loop, K5; rep from * to last 4 sts, P1 through back loop, K3.

Row 2 (right side): P3, *K1 through back loop, P5; rep from * to last 4 sts, K1 through back loop, P3.

Row 3: Rep Row 1.

Row 4: Rep Row 2.

Row 5: Rep Row 1.

Row 6: Rep Row 2.

Row 7: * P1 through back loop, K5; rep from * to last st, P1 through back loop.

Row 8: * K1 through back loop, P5; rep from * to last st, K1 through back loop.

Row 9: Rep Row 7.

Row 10: Rep Row 8.

Row 11: Rep Row 7.

Row 12: Rep Row 8.

Rep these 12 rows.

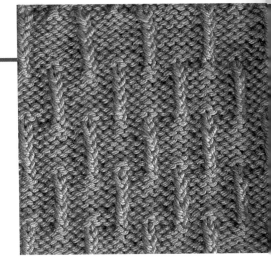

JUNE 16

Woven Cable Stitch

Multiple of 4

Row 1 (right side): *Cable 4 front; rep from * to end.
Row 2: Purl.
Row 3: K2, *cable 4 back; rep from * to last 2 sts, K2.
Row 4: Purl.
Rep these 4 rows.

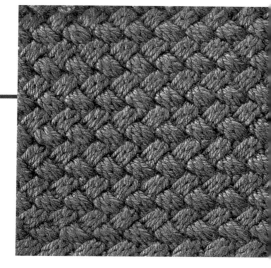

JULY
10

Horizontal Dash Stitch

Multiple of 10 + 6
Row 1 (right side): P6, *K4, P6; rep from * to end.
Row 2 and every even row: Purl.
Row 3: Knit.
Row 5: P1, *K4, P6; rep from * to last 5 sts, K4, P1.
Row 7: Knit.
Row 8: Rep Row 2.
Rep these 8 rows.

JUNE
17

Little Cable Stitch

Multiple of 6 + 2
Row 1 (right side): Knit.
Row 2: Purl.
Row 3: P2, *cross 2 back, cross 2 front, P2; rep from * to end.
Row 4: Purl.
Row 5: Knit.
Row 6: Purl.
Rep these 6 rows.

JULY
9

Squares

Multiple of 10 + 2
Row 1 (right side): Knit.
Row 2: Purl.
Row 3: K2, *P8, K2; rep from * to end.
Row 4: P2, *K8, P2; rep from * to end.
Row 5: K2, *P2, K4, P2, K2; rep from * to end.
Row 6: P2, *K2, P4, K2, P2; rep from * to end.
Row 7: Rep Row 5.
Row 8: Rep Row 6.
Row 9: Rep Row 5.
Row 10: Rep Row 6.
Row 11: Rep Row 3.
Row 12: Rep Row 4.
Rep these 12 rows.

JUNE
18

Rickrack Pattern

Multiple of 3 +1

Row 1 (right side): K1 through back loop, *M1, K2tog through back loop, K1 through back loop; rep from * to end.

Row 2: P1 through back loop, *P2, P1 through back loop; rep from * to end.

Row 3: K1 through back loop, *K2tog, M1, K1 through back loop; rep from * to end.

Row 4: Rep Row 2.

Rep these 4 rows.

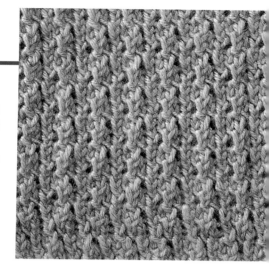

July
8

Checkerboard

Multiple of 8 + 4
Row 1: K4, *P4, K4; rep from * to end.
Row 2: P4, *K4, P4; rep from * to end.
Row 3: Rep Row 1.
Row 4: Rep Row 2.
Row 5: Rep Row 2.
Row 6: Rep Row 1.
Row 7: Rep Row 2.
Row 8: Rep Row 1.
Rep these 8 rows.

JUNE
19

Woven Horizontal Herringbone

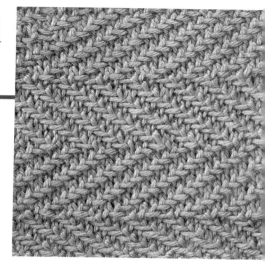

Multiple of 4

Row 1 (right side): K3, *sl 2 wyif, K2; rep from * to last st, K1.

Row 2: P2, *sl 2 wyib, P2; rep from * to last 2 sts, P2.

Row 3: K1, sl 2 wyif, *K2, sl 2 wyif; rep from * to last st, K1.

Row 4: P4, *sl 2 wyib, yf, P2; rep from * to end.

Rows 5–12: Rep Rows 1–4 twice.

Row 13: Rep Row 3.

Row 14: Rep Row 2.

Row 15: Rep Row 1.

Row 16: Rep Row 4.

Rows 17–24: Rep Rows 13–16 twice.

Rep these 24 rows.

JULY
7

Banded Basket Stitch

Multiple of 9 + 6
Row 1 (right side): P6, *K3, P6; rep from * to end.
Row 2: K6, *P3, K6; rep from * to end.
Row 3: Rep Row 1.
Row 4: Rep Row 2.
Row 5: Rep Row 1.
Row 6: Rep Row 2.
Row 7: Rep Row 2.
Row 8: Rep Row 1.
Row 9: Rep Row 2.
Row 10: Rep Row 1.
Rep these 10 rows.

JUNE
20

Embossed Check Stitch

Multiple of 2 + 1

Row 1 (right side): K1 through back loop; rep from * to end.

Row 2: K1, *P1 through back loop, K1; rep from * to end.

Row 3: P1, *K1 through back loop, P1; rep from * to end.

Row 4: Rep Row 2.

Row 5: Rep Row 1.

Row 6: P1 through back loop, *K1, P1 through back loop; rep from * to end.

Row 7: K1 through back loop, *P1, K1 through back loop; rep from * to end.

Row 8: Rep Row 6.

Rep these 8 rows.

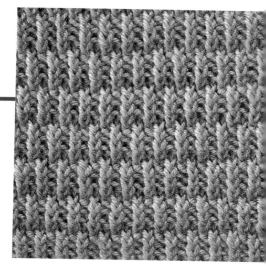

JULY
6

Large Basket Weave

Multiple of 6 + 2

Row 1 (right side): Knit.
Row 2: Purl.
Row 3: K2, *P4, K2; rep from * to end.
Row 4: P2, *K4, P2; rep from * to end.
Row 5: Rep Row 3.
Row 6: Rep Row 4.
Row 7: Knit.
Row 8: Purl.
Row 9: P3, *K2, P4; rep from * to last 5 sts, K2, P3.
Row 10: K3, *P2, K4; rep from * to last 5 sts, P2, K3.
Row 11: Rep Row 9.
Row 12: Rep Row 10.
Rep these 12 rows.

JUNE
21

Embossed Rib

Multiple of 6 + 2

Row 1 (right side): P2, *K1 through back loop, K1, P1, K1 through back loop, P2; rep from * to end.

Row 2: K2, *P1 through back loop, K1, P1, P1 through back loop, K2; rep from * to end.

Row 3: P2, *K1 through back loop, P1, K1, K1 through back loop, P2; rep from * to end.

Row 4: K2, *P1 through back loop, P1, K1, P1 through back loop, K2; rep from * to end.

Rep these 4 rows.

JULY
5

Fancy
Slip-Stitch Rib

Multiple of 5 + 2
Row 1 (right side): P2, *K1, sl 1, K1, P2; rep from * to end.
Row 2: K2, *P3, K2; rep from * to end.
Rep these 2 rows.

JUNE
22

Corded Rib

Multiple of 4 + 2

Row 1: K1, *K2tog through back loop, pick up horizontal strand of yarn lying between stitch just worked and next st and knit into back of it, P2; rep from * to last st, K1.

Rep this row.

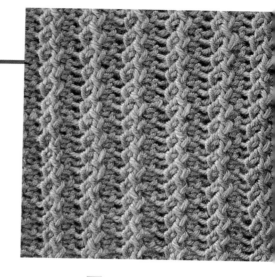

JULY
4

Supple Rib

Multiple of 2 + 1

Row 1 (right side): K1, *knit the next st but do not slip it off left-hand needle, then purl the same st and the next st tog, K1; rep from * to end.

Row 2: Purl.

Rep these 2 rows.

JUNE
23

Moss Rib

Multiple of 4 + 1
Row 1: K2, *P1, K3; rep from * to last 3 sts, P1, K2.
Row 2: P1, *K3, P1; rep from * to end.
Rep these 2 rows.

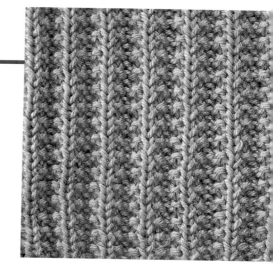

JULY
3

Uneven Rib

Multiple of 4 + 3
Row 1: *K2, P2; rep from * to last 3 sts, K2, P1.
Rep this row.

Open Chain Rib

Multiple of 6 + 2
Row 1: K2, *P4, K2; rep from * to end.
Row 2 (right side): P2, *K2tog, YO twice, sl 1, K1, psso, P2; rep from * to end.
Row 3: K2, *P1, purl into front of first YO, purl into back of 2nd YO, P1, K2; rep from * to end.
Row 4: P2, *YO, sl 1, K1, psso, K2tog, YO, P2; rep from * to end.
Rep these 4 rows.

JULY
2

Beaded Rib

Multiple of 5 + 2
Row 1 (right side): P2, *K1, P1, K1, P2; rep from * to end.
Row 2: K2, *P3, K2; rep from * to end.
Rep these 2 rows.

JUNE
25

Tweed Pattern

Multiple of 6 + 3
Row 1 (right side): K3, *P3, K3; rep from * to end.
Rows 2 and 3: Rep Row 1.
Row 4: Knit.
Row 5: Purl.
Row 6: Knit.
Rows 7, 8, and 9: Rep Row 1.
Row 10: Purl.
Row 11: Knit.
Row 12: Purl.
Rep these 12 rows.

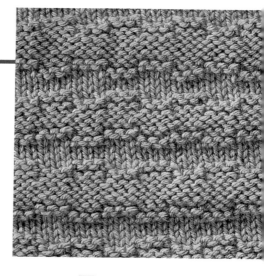

JULY
1

Farrow Rib

Multiple of 3 + 1
Row 1 (right side): *K2, P1; rep from * to last st, K1.
Row 2: P1, *K2, P1; rep from * to end.
Rep these 2 rows.

JUNE
26

Puffed Rib

Multiple of 3 + 2
Row 1 (right side): P2, *YO, K1, YO, P2; rep from * to end.
Row 2: K2, *P3, K2; rep from * to end.
Row 3: P2, *K3, P2; rep from * to end.
Row 4: K2, *P3tog, K2; rep from * to end.
Rep these 4 rows.

June
30

Stockinette Checks

Multiple of 10 + 5
Row 1 (right side): K5, *P5, K5; rep from * to end.
Row 2: P5, *K5, P5; rep from * to end.
Row 3: Rep Row 1.
Row 4: Rep Row 2.
Row 5: Rep Row 1.
Row 6: Rep Row 1.
Row 7: Rep Row 2.
Row 8: Rep Row 1.
Row 9: Rep Row 2.
Row 10: Rep Row 1.
Rep these 10 rows.

JUNE
27

Oblique Rib

Multiple of 4

Row 1 (right side): *K2, P2; rep from * to end.
Row 2: K1, *P2, K2; rep from * to last 3 sts, P2, K1.
Row 3: *P2, K2; rep from * to end.
Row 4: P1, *K2, P2; rep from * to last 3 sts, K2, P1.
Rep these 4 rows.

JUNE
29

Diagonal Seed Stitch

Multiple of 6
Row 1 (right side): *K5, P1; rep from * to end.
Row 2: P1,*K1, P5; rep from * to last 5 sts, K1, P4.
Row 3: K3, *P1, K5; rep from * to last 3 sts, P1, K2.
Row 4: P3, *K1, P5; rep from * to last 3 sts, K1, P2.
Row 5: K1, *P1, K5; rep from * to last 5 sts, P1, K4.
Row 6: *P5, K1; rep from * to end.
Rep these 6 rows.

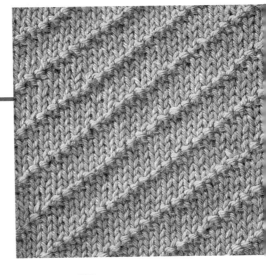

JUNE
28

Index

G

Goblets, December 29
Grand Eyelets, May 7
Granite Rib, April 20

H

Half Brioche Stitch, October 18
Half Fisherman's Rib, March 17
Harris-Tweed Rib, December 5
Herringbone, October 29
Herringbone Lace Rib, January 10
Hindu Pillar Stitch, December 15
Honeycomb Cable, August 6
Honeycomb Cable Stitch, December 28
Honeycomb Pattern, August 7
Honeycomb Stitch, December 20
Horizontal Dash Stitch, June 17
Horizontal Herringbone, October 30
Horizontal Ridge Stitch, February 17

Horizontal Two-One Ribs, February 23
Houndstooth Pattern, February 15
Houndstooth Tweed, July 27
Hourglass Eyelets, July 21
Hunter's Stitch, December 6

I

Interrupted Rib, March 26
Inverness Diamond, December 13

K

King Charles Brocade, December 12
Knit-One, Purl-One Rib, September 8
Knit-Two, Purl-Two Rib, September 9
Knot Pattern, December 19

Knot Stitch, September 12
Knotted Cable, August 10
Knotted Cords, January 22
Knotted Openwork, January 8
Knotted Rib, July 12

L

Lace and Cables, January 14
Lace Check, August 1
Lace Rib Panel, October 26
Lacy Bubbles, January 13
Lacy Checks, April 13
Lacy Diamonds, July 29
Lacy Openwork, November 10
Lacy Rib, January 5
Lacy Zigzag, November 1
Ladder Stitch, June 5
Large Basket Weave, June 21
Large Eyelet Rib, October 12